HAPPY EVER AFTERS
a storybook code to teaching
children about disability

HAPPY EVER AFTERS
a story book code to teaching children about disability

Kathy Saunders

Trentham Books

First published in 2000 by Trentham Books Limited

Trentham Books Limited
Westview House
734 London Road
Oakhill
Stoke on Trent
Staffordshire
England ST4 5NP

British Cataloguing in Publication Data
A catalogue record for this book is available from the
British Library
ISBN 1 85856 213 9

For further informtion:
http/web.ukonline.co.uk/happyeverafters

Designed and typeset by Trentham Print Design Ltd., Chester and printed in Great Britain by Cromwell Press, Trowbridge, Wiltshire

This is dedicated to Paul who made it possible, to Rosemary and Claire who made it important, and to Winnie's friends.

CONTENTS

Kathy Saunders was educated at a school for physically disabled children and took up a career in medical laboratory sciences before being blessed with two children. In *Happy Ever Afters*, she combines her personal experiences as a parent, school governor, classroom helper and children's book reviewer with her numerous disability contacts, to produce this guide to help teachers and parents explain how disability in real life often varies from its portrayal in the books their children read.

An audio version of this book is available to print disabled people. To order, telephone the Royal National Institute for the Blind (RNIB) Customer Services on 0345 02 3153.

INTRODUCTION

How do children learn about disability in society? A particular perspective is offered in an informal report *Families First* (1995). It is written by parents who are disabled and whose non-disabled children go to their local primary and secondary schools. This suggests that there is wide variation between schools and among individual teachers regarding the approach to disability as a community or cultural issue. It casts doubt on how many schools are aware of their part in creating attitudes about disability, and questions methods of teaching about disability itself, as distinct from those disability concerns which are recognised and expressed as students' educational special needs.

In addition, the report indicates major differences in approach to disability between families in which one or both parents had been disabled as children themselves compared with families where disability was suddenly introduced through illness or accident after their children were born. This suggests that dealing with disability has to be learned or conversely, that unhelpful attitudes need to be unlearned before non-disabled people and their families can progress to coping with disability.

There was evidence, too, that some young children encountered worrying comments from their peers and teachers. Some brought home new negative attitudes by picking up the disablist notions of the wider community and, it was thought, through some aspects of school resources, environment and teaching methods. This was particularly identifiable in the written word.

Famously, at least one in four people experience personal disability at any one time, but few individuals will survive a normal lifespan without experiencing some degree of disability in themselves, their family, friends or through their work. Most disabled people do not recognise themselves as part of a 'disability culture'. Only a third belong to disability interest groups, mainly to access information, and fewer still join welfare rights campaigns. The whole range of life styles is here, on which the impact of disability varies according to infinite combinations of people's individual conditions, age, emotional factors and economic status. However the expression of these variables, and the people who are involved with them at each facet and level, can be termed a culture.

Disability is not a cultural minority issue. It is a fundamental human experience which generally transcends all other social groupings, situations and activities, giving particular resonances to each underlying category.

Teachers are required to reflect their communities and to prepare children for the experiences of life. Why is it, then, that so much teaching about this fundamental experience seems to be off-centre, relegated to a piecemeal approach, or dependent on individual teachers?

Three possible reasons suggest themselves. First, a misconception that identifying Special Educational Needs (SEN) satisfies the cultural demands. Second, that it falls exclusively within the remit of Personal and Social Education (PSE) tutors. Third, that so few teachers feel confident to expand on how their subjects relate to disability.

This publication is not about SEN, though the attitudes it exposes go some way to explaining why SEN Co-ordinators' jobs are so frustrating. It's not even about PSE, though there are clear connections. Confidence in teaching about disability is gained through personal or taught expertise, and by developing ways to put the fundamental experience of disability in real-time context across the entire curriculum. Drawing children into age-appropriate discussions with suitably trained adults across the whole range of teaching will make disability issues more relevant to the life our children have to deal with as individuals now, and as a society when the predicted demographic changes render more of the population disabled.

We need to know how to prevent the absorption of subtle, unintended misinformation that prevails in many reading resources, texts and methods before it becomes consolidated into a taught, but ultimately unhelpful, attitude.

I have developed the DICSEY Code to provide a manageable six-point plan that uses the medium of picture book and story texts to illustrate how to bring control to the nebulous, diverse and conflicting strands of disability across the whole curriculum and through every resource. The method is simple, but the rationale, the basic awareness of 'need-to-do' will remain a challenge to many until they take this opportunity to view the presentation of their subjects from a different perspective.

Families First (1995) *A study of disabled parents of school-aged children and their families.* Published by the Association of Disabled Parents in the Norfolk Area (PANDA), ceased 1998. Copies are available from public libraries in West Norfolk and North Cambridgeshire, main County Libraries in the UK and the British Library.

PART ONE
Children, disability and fiction

To most people, teaching very young children about disability appears to be artificial political correctness, bedevilled by a lack of appropriate resources and time.

At primary school, children learn to recognise approval of ability and independence. The tolerance shown to those who depart from expected standards depends largely on their teacher's skill. An emphasis on 'helping', safety and healthy living to prevent disability sometimes directly conflicts with accepting disability, however superficially. A fairly extensive body of children's literature and text-books give subliminal or frankly negative messages about the supposed nature of people with disabilities, illnesses or differences, and this can be reinforced by the general absence of discussion about the subject.

Anecdotal evidence from parents who were disabled before their children are born suggests that there are noticeable differences in the attitudes towards disability shown by their offspring and by their peers for whom disability is not an accepted part of life. Many children do not become aware of disabled people until they join playgroups. Their questions and comments to the children who have disabled parents may simply show plain curiosity, which needs to be properly satisfied, but some will show uneasiness or reject the idea of such differences. This may be partly instinctive but also partly learned from their families and environments, where the idea of increasing abilities is naturally presented as paramount, but without informed qualification. This obvious contrast with disability can be unsettling. Many adults have not had an opportunity to learn how to identify visual and verbal factors in the environment which detract from encouraging in children a fair and constructive disposition towards disability and disabled people. The interface between children and the frequency and character of these factors will require more research to determine how greatly bias, learnt behaviour and the environment create and shape attitudes. This is critical in designing methods for managing disability issues.

Very early on, many children internalise a basic message that disability is a fearsome thing that happens to other people. The reality is that some young children find themselves personally involved, perhaps through becoming disabled themselves or by having parents, siblings or other close relatives and friends who are or become disabled. Often, these children discover the hard way that what they have learned about disability in the past has not prepared them for their present situations. They have to readjust their thoughts before they can begin to cope, and some may rightfully ask why they were so badly misled in the first place. Schools are by no means the only source of such misinformation but they do represent a potent means of encouraging children to be more critical about how these attitudes are created beyond their school gates, if only by challenging and eliminating the damaging attitudes children have assumed.

This book offers an alternative approach. There is readily available children's literature with story lines and illustrations which can be used and adapted so that positive concepts and coping strategies can be introduced to even the youngest children. It shows how some unhelpful ideas are reinforced by children's literature. This book argues that disability is about everyday life and that talking about it can be made a much easier, routine practice.

Where we start

We are becoming more adept at teaching children how to interpret texts that give negative and unhelpful portrayals of gender and race. Society as a whole is learning, slowly, that there are alternative ways of living. We know there are varying views to accommodate. In part, this is aided by the most obvious sexist and racist elements being rejected in the modern publication process. Teachers and readers of older books are more aware that these may contain archaic sentiments. They can happily analyse them with the benefit of hindsight, and dismiss them as remote from themselves. This is far less true of issues associated with disability, where attempts to analyse texts tend to be either simplistic or overlooked altogether.

Some analyses imply that negative texts should be censored or somehow removed from circulation. This is impossible even were it desirable. To a small extent they are useful as a focus for informed debate, but all too often discussion is curtailed by lack of time, failure to identify the negative implications, or simply unsuited to the classroom context of independent reading. Fluent readers may never be prompted to challenge disablist notions. Longer books may reveal an overall positive message only in the last few pages, so leaving negative messages for children who do not finish reading the story.

Techniques of criticism need to be established early, while children are still busy with picture books, because once they progress to independent reading there is so little opportunity to discuss longer texts in detail with individual readers or a whole class. The discussion of negative texts is crucial in itself, but it also presents a valuable resource for developing readers' oral skills and comprehension in a relevant context. Without discussion, lingering ideas can become consolidated into taboos by half-baked information and minimal personal experience. Stereotypes replace reality and are subsequently regurgitated for another generation. As discussion is not always possible, it becomes essential to ensure that resources are positive or at least neutral.

Why it is important to recognise disability bias

From a literary point of view, we need to widen our critical skills to improve communication and stimulate more versatile writing formats. Perceptions of the potency of image, in both text and illustration, need active help to make it easier to identify subliminal, often unintended messages which would otherwise pass unchallenged into the minds of the next generation of super-receptive young readers.

Children grow up with the message that 'books are good', but many books are riddled with ideas about disability which have no relevance in the modern world. As with swearing, graphic violence and frank sexuality, the medium of print lends authority to the perception that 'if it's in a book, it must be all right'. Desensitisation might occur long before a more measured view can be developed.

Why children need to know

Parents who have disabilities suspect that very young children do not recognise disability. Mum is Mum whether she is disabled or not. Rising threes and four year olds are deeply curious about people who look different and their questions about disability are often badly answered. Adults might be ignorant, embarrassed or both. They can fail to grasp the scope of a child's question. Sometimes they genuinely don't want to worry the child, but end up making matters worse. They may think the child too immature to understand or too young to form an opinion but there is a mounting body of research which indicates that young children are very familiar with the social conventions of their elders (Brown,1998).

The early years of school may reinforce acceptance of a physical environment which is hostile to disability. Implied references to disability tend to be negative. For example, a successful talk on road safety depends on instilling a fear of injury which goes beyond the actual pain. 'You might not walk again' is necessarily, in this context, the bottom line. We don't tell them how it is possible to manage without walking, because although equally important, it dilutes the more obvious message.

Social training at school may find itself expressed as fundraising for groups of disabled people. Raising money depends on creating a sense of difference and superiority of circumstance, concern or even, when superficially handled, pity. It is counterproductive, in this situation, to address the question of why the basic needs of some disabled people are neglected by their community as a whole. A natural consequence for young children is that they may develop a false sense that disability is about poor people who need everyone's help, or that it is adequately catered for.

Add to all of this the influence of reading books which present negative portrayals of disability, and a child will understandably form an overall impression that disability is remote as a possibility for themselves, and so lack empathy with people who are disabled. Absence of disability in all its shades may unintentionally create expectations in children of perfection. Such influences can have a significant affect on the way some non-disabled children think about their future:

- they may develop an exaggerated and incapacitating fear of relatively minor disabling conditions

- if they become disabled, they do not recognise themselves in the same terms as the disabled people they learned about. This can impose barriers to considering forms of assistance which could improve their quality of life

- if disabled, they may lose self-esteem or feel uncomfortable with their peers, or they may abandon progress towards independence and think someone else will cater for their needs

- they may reject careers in disability associated occupations, or fail to explore disability issues in whatever occupation they choose

- they may feel themselves to be unequal to the challenges which science imposes in antenatal care and parenting

- their views may compel them to neglect previously healthy relationships with friends who become disabled

- they may feel overburdened or even repulsed by taking on a minor caring role

- they may settle for a less than whole zeal to achieve their own potential because they see themselves as so much more able than others. They could fail to realise that life may demand more diverse skills in the future.

Who needs disability in children's fiction?

Adults need stories pitched at appropriate levels to help them talk to children about family members who have disabilities, or about disability in the community. Many parents who themselves have disabilities prefer to broach disability through this indirect route, but modern quality picture books and early readers involving disabled adults – other than grandparents – are rare. More elusive still are those whose adult disabled characters conduct their lives without undue problems and become role models for disabled and non-disabled children to reflect upon.

More stories are needed that deal with mental health disturbances and that combine ethnic minority characters and disability. Young disabled people of all backgrounds need to be able to see themselves as realistic characters in stories just like other children, and books that include such characters would provide useful support for discussions about the cumulative effects of more than one bias. Children who have potentially life-threatening conditions would also like to read stories which reflect their own situation but leave the character alive and relatively able at the end of the book.

Books that feature a disabled child character whose disability plays no part in the story are exceptionally useful. A good example of this 'just happens to be' approach is Michael Foreman's *Seal Surfer.* Pippa Goodhart's *Pest Friends* is a good second, where she almost but not absolutely ignores her heroine's disability. Both are described here in the mini-review section.

When assessing books by their cover notes, story lines that are appropriate for a given situation are often difficult to find. Some publishers avoid mentioning a disability interest on covers because, they claim, it kills books stone dead. However there are many well-written storylines that incorporate realistically described disabled characters which sell very well indeed, for example some of Michael Morpurgo's novels. Badly written stories will have a short life whether they have disability interest or not.

Some books seem to be misrepresented by the publisher's covers and can give misleading signals to potential readers. For example, Joost Drost's *Bubblegum Guy* (ISBN 0-7475-3125-0) is an easy reader fantasy about a boy who, from birth, spontaneously blows bubblegum bubbles when he gets angry. This simple tale could offer useful insight into the emotional maelstrom of behavioural difficulties, but the cover uninvitingly tells us the boy has a 'strange and unfortunate disability' till a solution to the 'weird problem' is found that 'breathes life into the special boy'. This blurb seems seriously short on street cred to attract readers among boys who may be experiencing difficulties with self-control.

Rachel Andersen's *The Bus People* was first published by Oxford University Press in 1989 (ISBN 0-19-27160-2). Maggie Palmer's jacket illustration offered a close-up of three solemn children. Pastel and grey hues clearly implied the harrowing nature of the text and would probably discourage children's attention. Each chapter is a cameo of the lives and thoughts of five severely disabled or disturbed children, showing how non-disabled adults react to them but fail to respond to their basic needs. There is no plot and little interaction between the children. These easy to read fictitious accounts lead even adults to gloss over the concealed questions, ignorant attitudes, sarcasm and injustice which the writer describes so precisely.

This quality of naked truth is Rachel Andersen's special skill, but even older children or adults might not understand that the text carries more truth than fiction. Most simply will not believe that the like of what Rachel Andersen describes really can happen.

Three years later, *The Bus People* was republished by Random Century in a Red Fox edition (ISBN 0-09-987420-2) with a new cover clearly intended to make it more child friendly. Liz Watkins dutifully draws smiley children playing in a sunny field with smiley Bertram the driver and smiley Mrs Lovegrove the escort. Its bright red cover invites young juniors to dip in – but they won't find daring schoolday adventures, not even the tame dags special-schoolers get up to. By implying an unfounded lightheartedness, this cover seems likely to mislead potential young readers in an opposite way to the original, trapping them in stories they do not have enough experience to evaluate adequately. *The Bus People* would be an excellent resource for guided disability awareness training for older children, parents, teachers and writers, but *The Famous Five* it is not.

Recent promotions of book and film associated merchandising have provoked concern, even disgust, at the insensitive models created of characters such as *The Hunchback of Notre Dame*. Bland adaptations of these classics have lost all the subtlety of the original text. The toys 'fix' visible disability as the only important feature of a character. They do great disservice to children, blocking the recognition of the complex diversity of human conditions and situations.

Message understood?

All fiction sends messages to its readers, but some are more easily understood than others. Disabled characters are best portrayed as having their own emotions and responding to circumstances as they occur. This contrasts with characters whose disability is seen only in terms of the responses they create in others. The better writers who feature disabled characters in situations that highlight disability ensure that their texts show the resulting emotions or consequences clearly and promptly. The disabling experience is not oversimplified or censored but placed in a broadly acceptable and realistic perspective.

Where the plot involves interaction between disabled and non-disabled characters or more than one disabled character, the predominant character's reactions should not be allowed to overwhelm or eliminate a fair exposition of the emotions of the others. This evidence makes it easier for readers to question the plot and try to solve dilemmas by drawing on the descriptions of the character's thoughts and combining it with their own experience, however limited that might be.

Several novels by Michael Morpurgo illuminate the experience of disability in a particularly accessible form for children. Within the plot, his everyday language crystallises minute intimate feelings rather than the more usual academic and impersonal treatment of disability 'rites'. In the complex plot of *The Ghost of Grania O'Malley*, for example, a TV report tells how Jessy, who is thought to be lost at sea, was rescued. The report included the disclosure that Jessy has cerebral palsy, to which Jessy responds 'Do they have to tell everyone about my lousy palsy? Do they?' Her reaction to the invasion of her privacy and the predictability of the media in highlighting a disability which had nothing to do with the news story was not essential for the plot, but it does give an important indication of Jessy's attitude – one echoed by disabled people in real life. Similarly, when Jessy is left out of the school outing, Morpurgo shows her anger burning holes in the page, yet keeps the disability issue controlled and does not let it overwhelm the plot.

Other authors use disability as a device to structure their plots or colour their characters but offer no realistic idea of the character's emotional response to their situations. This is more common in the 'classics' or their modern adaptations and will be examined in detail later.

Some texts create a picture of disability which is completely unreal, for example few women with speech impairments would have Ariel's trouble persuading the Prince to kiss them, as happens in *The Little*

Mermaid. Similar themes of compromised intimacy appear in *The Tin Soldier, Beauty and the Beast* and *The Hunchback of Notre Dame.* Young readers who have not had the kind of life experiences which might help them criticise these characters and plots cannot be expected to recognise such misrepresentation. There may be a connection between stories of this type and widespread misunderstanding of the normal sexual nature of disabled adolescents and adults, which can present as one of the most difficult disability-related problems that individuals and society have to face.

Even when they know they are reading fiction, children are encouraged to consider that all the components reflect real life. Unhelpful attitudes are absorbed as perfectly reasonable, correct and universally held. Young people will not understand the full significance of subliminal negative attitudes unless a more knowledgeable person helps them to do so. Comprehension must also include an understanding that books reflect the limitations, as well as the range, of an author's experience and skill.

The present book makes no claim to demonstrate supposed 'failings' or 'errors of judgement' by any author but simply tries to highlight factors which are currently regarded as so commonplace that they fail to arouse general comment – even though they can be so damaging. Once a book is published, there are no right or wrong interpretations, only opinions held by individual readers in light of their own perspectives. Nobody can confidently predict or control the reaction of an unknown audience. Any reader, child or adult, has the ability to mentally transform the work into something quite different from what the author originally intended. In most cases we are unaware this has happened, because normally we don't ask. This can lead to apparently conflicting views about disability in literature, each view being held to be the more accurate or meaningful by different observers who have different perspectives. We accept that general literary criticism will vary among individual critics, but when reviews that focus on an author's treatment of disabled characters contradict each other, it can confuse readers who are insufficiently familiar with disability to make a judgement for themselves. Use of a standard framework that addresses modern disability awareness, such as the one provided here, might help to guide authors and critics in evaluating disability issues separately from the effects of style, and so give an added dimension to the writing.

The book aims to provide interpretation from a generalised disability perspective and to show how a young reader might take up unhelpful ideas, many of which the writer almost certainly did not intend or possibly even know about. Some reviews given in Part Four show how literary criticism can be extended to include these factors and indicate how slight changes to the plot, descriptions or dialogue might transform an ambiguous story from unhelpful to constructive or at least neutral.

Whose story is it?

Disability is a vast subject, one which arouses widely differing emotions according to circumstances. Many authors select one main character through whom to tell one side of a story. Disability affects the whole society or family and not just the person with a condition, so it may be necessary to discuss the wider picture, using several complementary stories to illustrate a range of perspectives, especially in picture books, or to structure discussions so as to ensure a rounded appreciation of broader issues.

Reverse Images

A reverse image occurs when emotions that are aroused by descriptions or illustrations of fictitious characters become associated with real people. A hunched, astigmatic, knobbly-jointed, scarred, bloodshot-faced chap handing out goodies in the local playground raises hair on the back of readers' necks. As adult readers, we relish these impressions as portents of disaster. Children are sometimes encouraged to use images like these to colour their stories, but often we do not tell them how to find ways of creating tension without using notions of disability.

The real danger is that reverse images have a powerful message. Let children think hunched, astigmatic, knobbly people are a source of danger and suddenly children hesitate about perfectly ordinary people who have scoliosis, sight impairments or arthritis. What is worse, they fear the causal condition itself, not because of possible discomfort but because of its social effects. In addition, even as adults, we are led into failing to identify and adequately support people who have invisible disabilities, particularly mental health disturbances.

This confuses children's sense of trust. Try dressing the playground chap in a red hooded coat. Give him a white beard and a sack of presents. Relax, feel a warming calm – but is it justified? Too late! Readers' perceptions stick like treacle on Monday's school jumper.

Ahoy there, Illustrators!

Some children think anyone using an eyepatch is a dubious companion because almost every pirate in children's fiction has one, as well as an artificial limb following amputation. A penetrating and aggressive form of body language beams out from the uncovered eye. The hand hook gleams menacingly and – watch out – that crutch will clout you one! The stereotyped pirate is cruel, greedy and unsociable, an echo of *Treasure Island's* Long John Silver and *Peter Pan's* Captain Hook. In Pat Hutchins' 1989 early reader picture book *One Eyed Jake* (ISBN 0-370-30773), Jake has a 'horrible face, a terrible voice and an awful temper. Nobody liked him.' Jake's one-eyedness is not referred to again, nor is it relevant to the story. Contrast this with Margaret Mahy's 1995 *The Man Whose Mother was a Pirate*, in which Margaret Chamberlain's illustrations show an exuberant friendly pirate with an apparently full complement of working parts, but whose fancy to travel in a wheelbarrow just hints at the possibilities.

Let's get it right. Seamen of old had dangerous jobs, just like many other workers. Before antibiotics, severe injuries meant immediate amputations that were preferable to lingering gangrenous deaths. If they survived the butchery, most people continued their jobs or made a living some other way, if necessary by adapting the usual methods to their own needs.

Before marine chronometers, sailors plotted their positions at sea by viewing the sun through a variety of lenses. In time, concentrated light destroyed their sight but light still caused eye pain which patches would ease. Long John Silver isn't described as using an eyepatch, because he was a ship's cook and not responsible for setting a course, but Nelson used one to prevent excess strain to his remaining eye after a head injury slashed through his eyeball and probably caused his retina to detatch. He had also lost his hair through environmental poisoning, lost his teeth through scurvy, lost one arm from shrapnel through his elbow, survived abdominal injuries and had periods of depression, but at the time England needed a hero. Political spin is not new, so the reality of living through and beyond the carnage of naval battles was concealed, providing authors with a sanitised version to write about ever since.

Discussions about *Treasure Island*, *Peter Pan* and similar tales would constructively include prevention of industrial injuries, eye safety, proper use of antibiotics in modern healthcare, design and use of robotic prostheses, the history of travel and discrimination in employment. Not many visually impaired amputees are in today's military or marine services, so let's hope there's not another Trafalgar.

Use the pictures

There are several great advantages to using illustrated rather than all-text presentations. One is accessibility, both in terms of complexity for very young children, and in the classroom context of joint discussion. Even older students can be persuaded to read them if it is suggested that they are examined to see if they are suitable for younger children. And some cartoon format books are actually aimed at older children.

Pictures can portray disability images that are free of complicated textual explanations, for example in Michael Foreman's *Seal Surfer* or Verna Wilkin's *Boots for a Bridesmaid*. These show disabled characters doing everyday things without any indication of literary motive regarding the story line, although they have been deliberately put there by the writers. This is a splendid way out of the stereotyping debate, particularly as portraying the 'ordinariness' of disabled characters in text-only stories can be difficult. Inevitably, questions arise about the author's motives in including such a character, because most people still expect there to be some literary reason. Picture books allow for wider interpretation.

The sophistication that young children can bring to social discussions when prompted by picture books is examined in *Not So Simple Picture Books* (1994). Here Pam Baddeley and Chris Eddershaw clearly show that children are able to interpret and extend storylines well beyond their currently accepted attainment targets when guided by appropriately trained adults. A need to include these considerations in playgroups and nurseries is indicated in Babette Brown's *Unlearning Discrimination in the Early Years* (1998). Although not specifically addressed, the wider issue of disability could be introduced into the approach for under fives typified by Christine Moorcroft in *Responding to Stories* (1998). The philosophical concepts appear ambitious for three-year olds, but this is simply an extension of what very young children do all the time. Their relationship with their toys has all the ingredients for these discussions, provided their natural instincts are recognised and valued. There is no magic age for the transformation to 'adult' concerns.

Illustrations can show body language and emotion through minor changes in stance, gesture and facial features and expression. Perfectly happy characters can appear anxious or inadequate by shifting an eyebrow, letting a sock sag or leaving buttons undone, and even unfashionable patterns on clothes fabrics play a part in creating a character image. Spectacles, in particular, are a potent tool for suggesting that characters are wise, capable, scary, domineering or gullible, simply by altering the frames and size of eyes seen through the lenses. In *Pictures on the Page* (1990), Judith Graham analyses the interpretation of various illustrating techniques.

Detailed illustrations of homes, shops and forms of transport etc. can also help focus discussions about disability issues. Particularly useful examples for this are *Winnie the Witch* illustrated by Korky Paul, with text by Valerie Thomas; *Boots for a Bridesmaid* by Verna Wilkins, illustrated by Pamela Venus; Derek Brazell's illustrations in Bernard Ashley's *Cleversticks*; and *Helpers* by Shirley Hughes. All are discussed in the detailed reviews in Part Four.

Ask children about alternatives to steps. Are there pictures showing ramps or the wheelchair man logo? If not, why not? Is there a hearing loop or sympathetic hearing scheme sign, and what does it mean? Why are parking spaces for disabled drivers always close to buildings? Why are there lights and bleepers, tactile pavements and dropped kerbs on road crossings? Who else finds them useful? What else do we need to know about crossing roads? How many different ways are there to eat food, carry items, do up clothes, find information or move things about? How would Winnie the witch hang up her washing on the clothes line that's strung up between the chimneys and how many ways are there to dry clothes if you haven't a flying broom handy? Ask 'how else could we..?' and push imagination to its limits.

Develop and acknowledge the oddball theory that might just work, using whatever science/ history/ geography topic is being studied, even if Winnie ends up with magnets in her knickers that stick on metal clothes lines when she ejects them from a siege catapult made from palm trees! The possibilities of using this type of incidental approach are very wide, yet offer flexibility to adults who may want to focus attention on a narrower range of issues.

Picture book cartoon animals as fictional characters

Picture books which show cartoon animals or inanimate objects behaving with emotional responses like humans invite young readers to think about these characters as if they were simplistic humans. There is nowhere else for the imagination to go. This convention can serve a useful purpose by presenting single issues in an uncomplicated way and is now widely used as an entertaining vehicle to more fluent reading and extending vocabulary.

Some story lines work better than others because, within limits, analogy is accepted by small children. If the approach to the cartoon animal's activity breeches the generally applied limits of acceptance, there is a risk that even children who consciously determine that they are reading 'pretend' may take in or identify with the overall theme as if the cartoon animal were human.

An interesting comparison can be made between Rose Impey's *Precious Potter, the Heaviest Cat in the World,* illustrated by Shoo Rayner, and two other books: Jill Murphy's *Five Minutes Peace* and Martin Waddell's *You and Me, Little Bear,* illustrated by Barbara Firth. All are described in the detailed reviews that follow.

The difference in the complexity and tenor of the story lines is immediately apparent and reveals where the limits of acceptability are perhaps nudged too far by 'Precious'. He was born an underweight scrap of a kitten, tended by his mother to the exclusion of the rest of the family, until he becomes an exceptional heavyweight. He breaks all the equipment when he tries different jobs, and ends up as a famous attraction in a circus: the heaviest cat in the world.

Jill Murphy tells how tired Mrs. Large the elephant just wants a quiet bath, while Martin Waddell's little bear has to wait till his weary mum is ready to play. Both show animals performing human activity, but the scenarios are extremely familiar to all small children and within their likely scope of understanding.

Precious Potter is part of a series inspired by real record breaking animals and as such is an imaginative and humorous story for intermediate readers, but the book's length and seeming insensitivity produces another storyline, almost certainly unperceived by the author and perhaps only completely obvious to those involved with disability. Any child whose sibling has special needs and seems to be getting an undue share of parental attention, or whose parents have separated under the strain of badly addressed disability; any disabled young person on their umteenth job rejection or even a child who thinks themselves too generously proportioned, would interpret this book differently.

For them, the story crosses into personal experience, evidenced by their own feelings and those they perceive in others, such as the low value some people place on children with special needs. It does not acknowledge the strain that occurs when family members have not learnt how to cope fairly within the family and strangers do not understand the situation. It mocks the difficulty disabled people find in getting work, and the image of people who do not conform to the narrow, socially constructed norm. It has a supposedly happy ending, but its underlying ideas are as potent as can be in terms of seeding unhelpful notions about the imagined situation of people with disabilities and their families. It is not constructive for those who will become involved in similar situations in the future. Teachers with time to discuss this story with their pupils may pick up on greed, selfishness and the eventual success – of a kind – but it would take a counselling session to ensure that other ideas had been adequately addressed.

John Burningham's *Cannonball Simp* is similar in length to *Precious Potter* and is also a story of a rejected runt who ends up in a circus. At first Simp is portrayed as fearful and sad he but rapidly gains control of his situation through his own resourcefulness. Here too, the character's physical stature is used, but in a positive way. He is just the right size to act as a cannonball and he uses this to save the job of a clown who befriends him. He is immediately accepted as an equal part of the team. 'Precious' satisfies only the voyeuristic appetite of his audience: there is no suggestion that he will ever be appreciated for any other quality.

Circus stories abound with characters who have unusual abilities or appearance, and they are often depicted as subject to exploitation through their fear of starvation for want of alternative livelihoods. This may have been the situation for some in the past, but the very role of clown may obscure the possibility that the same people could be dynamic managers or owners of their circus business. The critical element is whether they can exercise free choice.

Cartoon animal stories must conform to the same parameters of acceptability that we apply to fiction about human beings. Even in 'fun fiction', children have a right to expect not to be misled about situations in which they may have to make a personal response in later life.

Get real with the Classics

Classics may be defined as books which stand out from their contemporaries due to merit of style, plot, characterisation, imaginative use of language or precision of observation. Classics may also present views which are considered typical of or controversial for their time, or provide an unusual perspective within their zones of circulation. They are not necessarily of a particular era, but it is the older books that tend to be recommended to successive generations. Some adults have difficulty recognising disabled characters in the books they read as children, as these elements were not highlighted for them at that time. This carries a risk that what was judged outstanding for a past generation remains so to generations who have changed social expectations. In addition, shifts in the use of language can obscure the original merit, and preserve out-dated phrases and forms of address.

For children to realise the value of some of the traditional icons of literature – many of which were not written for children – they must be helped to identify the differences in social circumstances and attitudes which they will find implied or plainly described. Classics depict many situations in which there have been dramatic changes in our approach to illness and disability. For example, modern advances in the control of infectious diseases have so greatly revolutionised everyday life that the severity of those diseases is sometimes forgotten, along with the continuing need to practice what we have learned.

However, this implies that these classics reflected the common attitudes of their time and this is not always the case. Often authors were themselves unusual in that they were highly literate and had time to write fiction which they generally wanted to publish. Personal bias or limited experience may have contributed to less than accurate representations. Then, as now, a colourful or heart-tugging portrayal of a disabled character was better than real life. Ordinary disabled people going about their lives in an unremarkable way were as unattractive as fictional characters to past authors as they are to today's writers. However misleading they may be now, these texts remain the source of the literary stereotype of disability.

Modern editions of classics or adaptations for children introduce further variables. Modernising and simplifying the original texts to facilitate readability can significantly reduce or obscure the very quality that made the book outstanding, though the result could be perfectly acceptable as reading material.

For their disability messages to today's young readers, classics and their adaptations must be considered independently of one another, because no child is likely to read the original alongside an adaptation. The essentially literary concerns of comparing new versions to the original are not as important here as the overall effect of adaptation in divorcing the disability interest from its social context as originally described. This can give a disembodied, heightened profile to a character's disabilities, and it is more open to an interpretation which fails to incorporate an awareness of the social responses of the time the story was set, or even of the present day. A brief examination of two classics and a random selection of their adaptations will highlight some of the difficulties involved. A more extensive analysis is presented in Pat Pinset's *Children's Literature and the Politics of Equality* (1997).

Treasure Island was first published in 1883, and was set in the 1750s, nearly a hundred years before Robert Louis Stevenson was born, in an age dominated by sea-borne warriors, and when vast fortunes awaited those explorers resourceful enough to grab them. The eighty-thousand word original (1984 Puffin edition ISBN 0-14-135016-0) was reduced to seven thousand in Ladybird Classic's 1979 retelling by Joyce Faraday, with illustrations by Dennis Manton (ISBN 0-7214-0597-5), and to four thousand by Beryl Johnston in the 1993 Grandreams edition illustrated by Stephen Walsh (ISBN 1-85830-016-9).

The most obvious disability concern here is that the two wicked villains are disabled, without a balancing villainy among the non-disabled characters. The original relates that Blind Pew and Long John Silver were both disabled 'in the King's service' when a cannon-shot pierced their ship in a sea battle. The naive Squire Trelawney engages Silver on his treasure hunt partly because he thinks it unjust that Silver has no war pension to live on.

Blind Pew opens the story, hesitatingly tap-tapping along an unfamiliar road at dusk, with his green shade over his face and a huge black seaman's cape making him look hunched and deformed. Nobody else was brave enough to deliver a death threat to the alcoholic former fellow-crewman Billy Bones. Young Jim Hawkins is pressed into guiding the 'horrible, soft-spoken eyeless creature... whose voice turns cruel, cold and ugly', and who, having delivered the Black Spot, 'skipped out of the parlour with incredible accuracy and nimbleness'. This seeming ability is challenged again when Blind Pew returns at night, sneers at his thuggish colleagues for the fear that prevents them finding more riches, then ignominiously falls into a ditch. More, he manages to climb out but is fatally injured by the customsmen's horses that he had clearly heard some distance away. In this situation even the youngest readers would have kept their heads down, and might judge Pew a tad unwise, but Pew is dispensable in the plot.

This theme of conflicting messages about abilities creates a tingle of uncertainty. It associates Pew's 'blindness' with not 'seeing' or realising the consequences of his actions, and hence lack of intellect. A sighted Pew would not have had the same effect and he arouses little sympathy because his frustration is shown as a cruel streak. He's a rat, and not a sensible one, so good riddance.

There are more conflicting messages when strong Long John Silver hops around a lurching ship with his crutch slung round his neck, cooking wondrous meals while plotting death to any who cross him. On land he murders in cold blood by throwing his crutch at a man's back, then he hops nimbly through tropical undergrowth to stab the fallen body. He seems able to move quickly over this difficult terrain without his crutch but he struggles on sand and rocky ground at points in the story where his leadership is challenged. Here, as with Pew, the reader is discomforted by a failure to establish the 'goalposts' of the character's ability.

In reality, people with mobility impairments often put aside their walking aids when they are in confined spaces and have familiar surfaces to lean on. They might have more difficulty on soft or slippery surfaces but they would certainly be unlikely to rid themselves of a crutch when trying to cross undergrowth, even if they could keep their balance well enough to throw a missile in a straight line while standing on one leg.

In reality, some conditions are subject to variations which allow people to manage better at some times than at others. Visually impaired people might cope better with some light than with none if they are partially sighted, rather than completely blind. In theory, there are some good examples of realism in the way that *Treasure Island's* disabled characters cope, but to over-emphasise this aspect is to miss the basic manipulation of disability as a tool in creating atmosphere and as a symbol for wickedness.

It is important for children to be taught that disability has no bearing on character. Disability can alter the framework in which various attributes are expressed, but it does not generate traits which did not exist before disability occured. Critically, it is the perception of the observer which changes in relation to their own previous experiences.

Blind Pew and Long John are natural leaders of men, although some would call them bullies. However foul Long John's deeds, readers are left with a sneaking admiration for the silver tongued con-man, the flash of adventure contrasting with the dour and dutiful doctor, the boring and superficial squire, and the ever-pardoned Jim. Stevenson's loveable rogue has superhuman abilities that were hard to imitate and he literally gets away with murder.

Both Blind Pew and Long John evoke a sense of unfairness in the reader, which could be expressed by the modern equivalent of: 'This rat has to be tolerated because he's disabled and to criticise seems to demean the complainant more than the villain, but he's pushing his luck to expect a pension paid for by the taxes of honest hardworking folk who deep down suspect he's not really as disabled as he looks. After all, he is able enough when he really wants to be, isn't he?' Would even Squire Trelawney's sense of justice remain robust if he realised Silver didn't reciprocate concern for his welfare?

Did Stevenson deliberately use Long John's 'bit of timber'? Maybe not. He may have been influenced by tales of a famous real-life privateer in the 1700s nick-named Pegleg because of his artificial leg. The author might have been seeking expression for his own bronchial condition, possibly TB, that affected him variously throughout his short life. He also wrote *The Strange Case of Dr. Jekyll and Mr. Hyde*, so he may have enjoyed the concept of linking variations of ability and character. More likely though, he simply observed and listened to the people around him. He put words to their prejudices and ignorance and found a theme to which readers still respond over a century later. We still ponder the nature of 'deserving' compared to previously agreed 'rights' and the limits of society's 'rights' to require a particular life-style in order to be 'deserving' of help.

The context of the times is largely lost in both adaptations. Neither mention Blind Pew's death; he just disappears leaving unanswered questions. The Ladybird version introduces the idea of 'old' Blind Pew, suggesting a modern stereotype of disability and age. The Grandreams illustration shows Blind Pew's hands and nails knobbly and elongated, and the eye contact is completely obscured, so producing a visual representation of fearsomeness. With the lack of development, the literary device served by these characters' disabilities is also lost. These versions offer no points of contact in modern experience and young readers are likely to conclude that the entire issue of disability is fictitious.

Examination of Johanna Spyri's *Heidi* (1880) is subject to translations from the original German, which is given no attribution in the Parragon 1994 edition (ISBN 1-85813-983X). This exemplifies the use of disability as a convenient vehicle for another message, in this case a semi-religious tract.

The 'invalid' Clara is obviously disabled, as is Peter's blind grand-mother, but Spyri also offers a brutally dismissive account of Heidi's mother's probable epilepsy and, confusingly, her death from emotional reaction to her husband's fatal accident, to explain how Heidi ends up with her Grandfather. Heidi's babysitter Ursel is criticised and dis-missed as 'stone-deaf'. Peter's learning and behavioural difficulty pro-vides superficial logic for Clara's cure, when he destroys her wheel-chair in a temper tantrum, thus provoking her attempts to walk.

Spyri did not engage in literary tricks. She urged a straight acceptance that a good, simple life and religious faith could moderate the effects of any difficulty if the individual made enough effort, and with the proviso that a greater power can determine what is best for us. Modern readers on all sides of spiritual debate may find this simplistic.

At first examination, *Heidi's* disability message is that Clara can only be completely happy when she is no longer disabled and, by inference of repeated reinforcement of spiritual messages, her new ability and happiness is due to following a particular religious philosophy. Para-doxically, there is no real conflict in the circumstances of Clara's 'cure'. Many disabled people who use wheelchairs can stand and walk – but not far enough to be useful. Some conditions will improve with gradual exercise, especially in childhood, but not necessarily enough to dispense with a wheelchair altogether. Nobody would accept leaning on other people's shoulders as a permanent alternative; they would prefer to use crutches.

The real problem here is Spyri's portrayal of disability as all-or-noth-ing, without acknowledging any of the range of abilities in which choice plays a part in selecting the best method of dealing with parti-cular situations.

The 'cure' she relates is not a cure. It may be an improvement derived from rest and exercise, the relaxation of smothering over-protection allowing opportunity to experiment, or even a positive impulse to achieve an aim without being hindered by self-conscious fear of losing dignity. By the same reasoning, intermittent resumption of wheelchair use in such circumstances would not constitute failure. To imply a major permanent change had taken place by virtue of Heidi's goodness or a spiritual blessing is misleading, but it is not fair to criticise past reasoning in light of new information, even in fiction. The 'cure' was due to factors Spyri either didn't know about or chose to ignore so as to advance her overall aim. For children now, it is far more important to recognise the author's attitude than to argue about its origin.

Clara's pleasure at the prospect of more freedom is wholly understandable in her situation, but she is restricted more by her social arrangements and attitudes than by her disability. The only valid observation here is that Grandfather has to widen his doorway to allow the wheelchair to pass, and a need to examine Clara's privileged but impeded lifestyle.

Peter's grandmother seems to sit lonely and deprived, a receptor for Heidi's charitable goodies. Today, the need to control one's own life is recognised, at least in principle, by giving benefits to disabled people who can then determine their own priorities rather than being subject to someone else's initiative. But before society made this possible, charity was an essential and accepted part of living. Peter's discomfort with reading is portrayed as laziness, which can supposedly be banished by effort, supplemented with threats of bodily harm and fear of criticism. If only it were that easy, then or now. This rationalisation of learning difficulties and misrepresentation of mental illness, as also shown when Clara's housekeeper judges Heidi as mentally disturbed, is as erroneous and almost as prevalent today as it was in 1880.

By contrast, Beryl Johnston's 1993 adaptation (Grandreams ISBN 1-85830-016-9) concentrates more on Heidi's welfare. Illustrations by Jenny Press show Peter's grandmother more able to contribute to the family, and Peter's reading improves without the threats. There is no mention of Heidi's mother or Ursel, and Clara's improved walking is due to 'good sun and mountain air'. This message has an altogether lighter and less misleading touch.

Positive discrimination?

Perhaps one of the reasons there are relatively few accurately described disabled characters in fiction is confusion over what actually constitutes motive. There are bound to be situations where a character's disability provides enough motive for actions on which a plot could be based. Some people's disabilities do provide a focus for their bitterness and frustration. Some do inspire admiration from those who have not experienced the same challenges. Some do have a tough time. The essential difference depends on how much the author allows the character's own emotions to be revealed within the story line. If they are there only to provide a focus for someone else's charity, goodness, revulsion or fear; if they represent only separateness, strangeness, inability, hostility or submission, they are unlikely to stimulate useful reflection in any reader.

If descriptions supply enough information for a reader to consciously determine a character's disability, does the author encourage us to dismiss them as irrelevant, or to analyse the portrayal of character and situation in a modern, constructive context? Modern welfare systems have robbed today's authors of easily categorised characters, but beware! There are some who say 'This is fiction and what was good enough for Dickens…'

We need not even go back as far as Victorian times. The advent of new technology has significantly changed the reality of life for some disabled people, as is evident when comparing books published at the present time with those written only a decade ago. For example, Hannah Cole's 1990 *In at the Shallow End* and Jamila Gavin's 1996 *The Wormholers* each features a child severely affected by cerebral palsy, but there is a major shift of attitude from subjection to enablement between them (see reviews).

Classroom resources

Look carefully at the reading schemes and factual texts in your classroom. References to disability are becoming more frequent in newer publications but are they appropriate in terms of questioning stereotypes and prompting children to think about alternative ways of living or do they consolidate unhelpful attitudes? Are they meaningful or tokenistic? If disability is not mentioned, how might its absence be interpreted?

A pupil's classroom experience is more than words on a page. It offers a superb opportunity to explore, discuss, reason and learn, but how many teachers have enough experience or training to confidently identify and use these sometimes ambiguous resources as pointers to a wider understanding of disability? Given that ability, is enough time allowed in tight teaching schedules to ensure adequate discussion of disability issues as an integral part of the lesson? Wouldn't it be easier if references to disability in recommended resources were thought through more holistically?

There is no subject which does not have a connection with disability issues, but it is reasonable for teachers to expect that their efforts to include discussions about these important life skills are not foiled by inadequate training, narrowly considered resources or counterproductive repetition across the entire curriculum. Use of the DICSEY Code may help to address some of those concerns.

PART TWO
Words we use

The use of language changes rapidly and there is much confusion about the preferred words to use when talking about disability. It is important to recognise how meanings differ, and to know why some terms are considered unhelpful.

The current World Health Organization definitions are:

Impairment is a physical deviation from the usual structure, function or development.

Disability is any restriction or lack of ability, due to an impairment, to perform an activity in the manner or within the range considered normal for a human being.

Handicap is a function of the relationship between disabled persons and their environment. Handicap is the loss or limitation of opportunities to take part in the life of the community on an equal level with others.

'Condition' is the medical description of the impairment. For example, if the impairment is a specific medical condition which causes blindness, then according to the WHO definition, the person's disability is not being able to see in the same way as most other people. Their handicap may be finding newsprint difficult to decipher.

Cultural forces have modified these definitions in some countries. In the UK, the term 'handicapped' is offensive to some people who associate it with begging (cap in hand) and the social implications of being thought unable to look after or provide gainfully for themselves. It remains broadly acceptable in some other English speaking countries and occurs in their modern literature.

The definition of impairment is the same in the UK, but 'disability' has developed the additional meaning of 'the limitation of opportunities caused by environmental or social organization'. This gives rise to two uses of the terms disabled and disability. The first, and currently the most common use of disabled and disability in the UK, is called the *medical model* of disability and means 'restriction due to an impairment'. The second and preferred use is that the environment disables people who have impairments, and this is called the *social model* of disability.

In terms of the first definition, the medical model, a person who cannot walk is disabled, and the inability to get up stairs with their wheelchair is due to their having to use a wheelchair. The problems arise with the person who has a specific impairment, such as cerebral palsy. This is a medical model of disability because it focuses on the person's condition and not on the lack of appropriate design and social arrangements in the environment. With the medical model of disability, many remedies depend on medical intervention, such as corrective surgery, which is expensive, not always successful, carries risk and can benefit only one individual.

According to the second definition, the social model, a person who uses a wheelchair is disabled by the absence of ramps and lifts. The impairment is a private matter between the person and their medical advisor, and the condition itself is irrelevant. A solution is to install a ramp which will benefit any number of people on a permanent basis whether they are disabled or not, such as those using shopping trolleys or babies' pushchairs. Here 'disability' describes the social barriers which prevent equality of opportunity and is developed further to describe a form of social oppression which can be overcome by social change.

Ultimately, using words which imply that disability describes personal medical conditions rather than social barriers will hinder the development of a fully inclusive society. Some campaigners consider that this includes phrases like 'people with disabilities' because this suggests that people 'own' medical conditions that disable them, rather than that they are disabled by unsuitable social arrangements. They extend this to define society as disabled, rather than the individual, in that it is society that is not organised adequately. This leads to a preference for the description 'disabled people'. Others think 'people with disabilities' emphasises that an individual person is much more important and should not be preceded or categorised by disability. Both arguments are valid within different contexts. 'Disabled people' looks towards long term social change while 'people with disabilities' reflects an immediate need for individuals to retain their identity.

However, in the UK most people currently use 'people with disabilities' as an acceptable alternative to 'disabled people' with no generally held understanding of how the terms are considered to differ, or with intention to make this distinction. There is a vague perception that some disabled people are adamantly of one opinion or the other and this gives rise to an uncertainty which saps confidence when attempting to talk about disability.

Both terms are used in this book because for teaching to be meaningful to young children it must work forward from a point that children will find familiar. It must also accurately explain the conditions that children see around them. Inevitably, this starts from the traditional medical model but teachers should introduce children to the concepts of the social model and be alert to more generally accepted shifts of meaning in the future. An eventual understanding of disability as a political issue will be better achieved when children reach maturity with well informed, positive attitudes.

'Normal' meaning 'not disabled' implies that anyone who has a disability is abnormal. Both descriptions are misleading because nobody is completely one or the other. 'Non-disabled', is preferred to describe people who do not have disabilities. 'Differently-abled' is sometimes used to describe disability but it is ambiguous. Invalid means 'not valid'.

Avoid the disabled!

The principle aim of talking about disability is to develop a sense of variety and individuality. 'The' disabled', 'the' blind', 'the' deaf are examples of terms which put all people disabled by similar conditions into one dehumanising stereotype. These terms reduce our capacity to invent and identify suitable choices for individual people with their unique impairments. 'People who are' disabled, blind or hearing impaired etc. is preferred. It is impolite to describe people as if they are their conditions. 'People who have arthritis' is preferred to 'arthritics'; 'people who have had polio' to 'polio people'.

A good rule is to put people first, and their condition, if it is relevant and not just being nosy, afterwards. In most cases, the disability definition will suffice: for example, a person with a mobility, hearing or visual impairment. Knowing someone has arthritis does not explain how that person is affected. It is like knowing someone banks with Barclays without knowing how much they have in their account.

If there is good reason to broadcast the private medical business of other people, use a neutral term, for example, a person who has/ with / who experiences/ developed a learning impairment. Here the person remains the most important part of the combination, and not merely an impotent subject of an all-conquering disabling force.

'Victim of' and 'crippled by' are not only misleading and inaccurate but also carry a social message and say that everyone who has a particular condition is the same. 'Crippled' means unable to do anything and needing rescue, like powerless ships at sea. 'Afflicted by' and 'suffering from' presumes knowledge of an individual that is more properly the province of confidential medical consultation. Disabling conditions often cause no pain in themselves or are managed by pain control techniques. The majority of people who need to take medicines for their condition have an illness which may or may not be the cause of their disability.

When society encounters conditions it cannot understand, it creates descriptive words which linger in the vocabulary long after more accurate and less prejudiced terms are developed. Each time these hostile terms are used, an unhelpful view is reinforced in the user as well as possibly offending the subject. This is especially true of conditions that affect the intellect and the mind. The descriptions are found widely in older literature, in modern texts referring to historical events, in some modern children's books and in most playgrounds.

'Mentally handicapped' is still commonly used in the UK, but 'people who have learning difficulties' or 'developmental disabilities' is preferable. Words like backward, dullard, oaf, retarded, idiot, imbecile, nit-witted and feeble-minded are used as insults.

People who have not experienced mental disturbances have coined a host of terms for those who have. Raving mad, crazy, barmy, maniac, insane, lunatic are so widely accepted in our language that they have come to mean 'someone who is doing something that someone else does not understand or agree with', as well as denoting various degrees of anger. 'Possessed' means possessed by evil or the Devil and is related to the belief that disabling conditions are a punishment for sins, now or in previous generations.

Examples in modern children's fiction are Lisa Taylor's *A Pig Called Shrimp*, Robert Swindell's *You Can't Say I'm Crazy* and Michael Morpurgo's *Mad Miss Marney*. Each uses the casual terms differently but the stories are actually about mystery and ignorance, not mental illness. They are all discussed in the mini-review section. Hilary McKay's *Dolphin Luck* offers scope to probe more deeply into this extensive area and is considered in the detailed reviews.

Mental illness is preferably called a mental health disturbance or a mental health problem. These descriptions are more accurate and respectful. Many of the symptoms experienced in most types of mental health disturbances can now be alleviated by medication, but some people experience severe side effects with these medicines. The term 'chemical prisoners' can be used to describe the situation of those adversely affected by medication but who are nevertheless required to take it so that they can live in the community without constant medical supervision. It indicates that current medications for mental health disturbances require a good deal more research to improve them and that the very best must be made available to all who need them.

PART THREE
The DICSEY Code, a framework for evaluation

The DICSEY disability awareness code has been designed to provide a framework for evaluating texts for disability issues. It sets out six major elements of disability awareness in the simplest terms, arranged so that the first letter of each element forms the mnemonic 'DICSEY'.

Each element is followed by more detailed notes intended as a guide for adults. Simple language is used wherever possible, to help adults make the issues more accessible for younger children. There is scope to pitch discussions appropriately for more mature children by drawing on points which discuss the issues that are of greater relevance to adults who work with children.

Examples of how the DICSEY code can be applied to fiction are given in the detailed reviews of individual books in Part Four. Its principles can be applied to almost any printed material and extended, if wished, to other formats.

THE DICSEY CODE

Disability Image Control Society Enabled Young carers

Disability   Disability affects us all. We can find new ways to do things.

Images   Images come from stories and pictures which only tell us part of the truth.

Control   Disabled people want to choose how to manage their own lives.

Society   We all make the rules of our society and we can change them to make it easier for everyone to take part.

Enabled   Disabled people need an environment which lets them do things for themselves.

Young carers   Everybody cares about their families. When someone close is ill or very disabled we may be worried, or help at home and look after ourselves more than our school friends usually do. It may affect our schoolwork and friendships. If this worries you, tell your parents or a teacher.

D – Disability
Disability affects us all.
We can find new ways to do things.

Disability is not an illness

A person is disabled if it is hard for them to do things in the same way as most other people because some part of their body works differently. Other ways are better for them. For example, a person whose leg is broken finds it hard to move around. A new way to move around is to use a wheelchair – which is easier if there are no steps to stop them. Disability tells us how people live part of their lives, not if they feel well or poorly.

Disability can be caused by an illness or accident

A person is disabled when they have an illness or accident which damages their body. The person will be disabled until their body can repair the damage, but if they are damaged too much to heal properly, some disability will remain after the illness is over. Healthy people heal better than less healthy ones and young people heal faster than older people. Most disabled people have had some sort of illness or accident. They use their other abilities to find new ways to do things.

Disability is not contagious

Most infectious diseases which led to disability in the past can now be controlled by immunisation (e.g. polio or measles), or vaccines are being developed or sought (e.g. AIDS). Non-infectious conditions which can also lead to disability include disorders of internal organs such as heart, kidney, lung or brain.

Conditions can be present at birth (e.g. Spina bifida or Down's syndrome). They can develop during life (e.g. diabetes or cancer), sometimes through poor nutrition or living conditions (e.g. rickets), or be caused by allergies or pollution (e.g. asthma).

Older people are more likely to have had accidents or illnesses and are less able to maintain healthy bodies than younger people because of the natural process of ageing. There is a greater chance that there will be some form of disability as age increases, but advancing age itself does not cause disability and there are many elderly people who are not disabled.

Various forms of brain damage or unusual patterns of development cause learning disabilities but most are only poorly understood at present. We know very little for certain about what causes most mental health disturbances. Some are thought to be due to unusual chemical activity in the brain.

Disability does not cause death

Sometimes the illnesses that can disable people make them so ill that their bodies do not have any chance to heal and they may die from their illness. Most disabled people live to old age.

Disability can be visible or invisible

Walking with sticks is a visible disability, deafness is invisible.

Disability is not caused by curses

Every culture has a system of spiritual or religious beliefs, from which some people develop significant emotional strengths. These can help to create positive lifestyles but they are wholly individual. Some conditions get worse if the disabled person gets very tired or worried, and may improve if the disabled person can be calm and positive. Traditional religious beliefs contribute to some wider cultural attitudes to disability.

Multiple disabilities reduce scope

Finding new ways of doing things depends on having other abilities to use. If these are also impaired, choices will be reduced, especially when sight, hearing or learning are involved. Many people with learning disabilities also have visual or hearing impairments. People with impairments of both sight and hearing are more challenged than people with either condition alone. People with mobility impairments become less mobile if their sight is reduced, because mobility becomes a conscious activity that relies on constantly checking paths for unevenness or obstructions. Minds and bodies that are more vigorous find new ways more easily.

Disability is not 'all or nothing'

Most people keep some of the function which is impaired, but its quality will change or reduce. Many blind people are 'partially sighted' – they can see some things, but not well enough to see everything they need to. We say 'visually impaired' to cover all situations. Hearing can be muffled or only effective for a small range of sound wavelengths. Mobility and dexterity can be impaired in terms of coordination, strength or stamina rather than by complete paralysis. Often only one system is affected. A person with impaired hearing is as likely as anyone else to have perfect sight and be a great athlete, but their speech may be impaired because hearing is part of the process which enables us to speak.

Brain damage or unusual development can cause anything from minor difficulties in reading to the need for constant relearning of everyday activities in small stages. Memory, personality and emotions might also be affected. Unusual development can favour alternative skills that can be advantageous if recognised and nurtured carefully.

Disability has no 'happy ever afters'

'Coming to terms' with disability refers to an emotional state in which a disabled person is supposed to have become accustomed being disabled, so that their lives are as satisfactory as anyone else's. This is a myth and misunderstands the basic nature of coping with disability.

People who have 'come to terms' have created a balance between what they want to do in their daily lives and what they can actually do, whether under their own steam, with aids or with more active enablement strategies. But lives and bodies continually change. People who seem to stay in control are in fact constantly revising and readjusting the balance of their lives in response to temporary and more permanent changes. They try to predict and take account of what might lie ahead. Their success depends on their psychological, emotional and financial means. For example, a person who walks reasonably on crutches is in balance until it snows. Another will develop a good working relationship with their usual personal assistant which may be impossible to replace quickly if the assistant is unavailable. Apparently minor changes can cause the balance to tip into difficulty and frustration, and unnecessary barriers are sometimes unabsorbable. It takes resource-fulness and perseverance, or an exceptionally static life style to 'come to terms' with disability for any substantial length of time.

Disability is OK?

Children are sometimes perplexed by the apparent contradiction between people saying disability is OK and trying hard to prevent it. Both approaches are true, depending on the context of the discussion. To a disabled person, being disabled is usually OK because, eventually, most people do cope adequately and find it's not as bad as they thought. It usually does not change their personalities or reduce their own perceptions of their self-worth in relationships with family, friends and society. People might find that having a disability prompts them to switch to different, though no less valuable, priorities but their inner essence is not altered in any significant way. They certainly meet people who approach them differently from the way they might if no disability were involved, and this is a highly complex social interaction for everyone concerned. Many disabled people find it difficult to influence and deal with such interactions, because it depends so heavily on the other person's instantaneous reaction to their first meeting, when they cannot know the essence of the disabled person, only the visible exterior.

Although appropriate for many people who have a disability, the 'it's OK' approach risks trivialising the effort that some have to put into merely coping. It can alienate those who find they don't have the resources they need in order to manage.

We try to prevent illnesses and accidents because people who become severely injured or ill could die, instead of recovering with a disability. Illness and disability have a high financial cost in our society. Prevention does not reflect a lower value to society of those who are disabled but a heightened estimate of the value of life itself. It also acknowledges the personal price of illness and disability to each individual in terms of possible discomfort, practical and emotional inconvenience, lack of choice, and financial loss in a society which does not always adequately accommodate individual needs.

Disability is unique

Everybody knows something about disability through their family, friends, work or in themselves. It is not only about what happens to our bodies but, more importantly, it is about how people behave towards each other and expect to have happy and satisfying lives. No two people will be exactly the same, but everyone can be aware of what will help or hinder the people they know who have disabilities, and what to aim for should they become disabled themselves.

I – Images
Images come from stories and pictures that only tell us part of the truth.

Images in books cannot be full descriptions

They are pictures of people or situations that leave out all the parts not wanted by the writer or artist. If we always see or hear the same image about a group of people, in time we come to believe this image to be how they are in real life. A stereotype is created. It is an author's 'short-cut' which saves writing a longer but fuller and more accurate description of a person that would tell the readers about their personality and circumstances.

Stereotyped disabled images

Characters with disabilities have been used in stories to create reactions of dislike, fear or pity in other characters or the reader. Examples are Captain Hook in *Peter Pan*, who had an amputated hand, Gollum in *Lord of the Rings* who was visually impaired, and Ariel in *The Little Mermaid*, whose lack of speech was an important aspect of the plot. These and many other stories could not have been written without exploiting an image of the disabled parts of these characters, but in real life there's more to consider.

Reverse images

Reverse images occur when readers absorb the emotion of dislike, fear or pity in fiction and mentally transfer it to real life disability or disabled people.

Images in popular media

Newspaper, magazine, radio and TV writers may think that their readers want short-cut characters, or they may be short of time or space to describe a person or event in accurate detail. They may lack experience, make assumptions or unthinkingly replicate existing stereotypes. Disabled people are often described as 'heroes' for doing perfectly ordinary things which are well within their capabilities, because the writer assumes disabled people are less able in everything. In real life, disabled people are seldom the tragic, poverty-stricken, powerless characters that some authors choose to write about.

Charity Images

In the past, charity appeals have used images of people with disabilities who appeared to be dependent on others, with no career prospects, no love life, no children of their own, no social life. These images were created to encourage donations, but they also made everyone think that all disabled people are like that. Many disabled people object to the concept and practice of providing life's essentials through charity.

Advertising images rarely use obviously disabled models, even when products are aimed at the 'disability market'. The absence of images of disabled people doing the same as everyone else makes some people doubt their ability to manage any disability in themselves or those close to them.

Stereotyped images are second-hand thoughts

Images affect every part of our lives, but it is important to understand that stereotyped images are always second-hand ideas generated by other people. They can help to raise our expectations, but they can also make us feel unequal to the picture they create of other people.

Images make us think we know more than we really do. They can stop us finding out for ourselves the whole truth about our own potential, abilities and needs, and those of everyone around us.

C – Control
Disabled people want to choose
how to manage their own lives

We all make choices about our lives

We decide what we like to eat, wear and how we manage our lives. When we're grown up we don't expect other people to have a say. Disabled people who get help in their daily lives can find that other people make choices for them or about them instead of asking what they prefer. Sometimes their choice is ignored or there may be no real options to choose from because they are told that what they want cannot be organised.

Often a disabled person cannot choose what sort of help would suit them best, or when it is given, because their helpers are employed to help several disabled people who all have different needs. The employer makes the decisions. This affects how each disabled person runs their homes, what they eat, when they get up and how late they can stay up in the evenings. If they use help to go out of the house, it has to be carefully planned in advance so that it suits the helper's timetable too.

Some helpers are paid

More disabled people are now given money to employ someone of their own choice. This allows them to change what they want from day to day and have more control over their lives.

Making decisions

Adults who have severe learning disabilities and some who have mental health disturbances may be considered incapable of making decisions about money or their own welfare, so responsibility is given to someone else, usually a relative. Many people with learning disabilities want more say in how their money is spent and how they live their lives. Sometimes people with learning disabilities and mental health disturbances can choose someone else to look after their interests and help them to change decisions if they do not agree with them. This person is called an advocate.

Some people find it more difficult to stay in control when the person who helps is a close relative. People whose needs are linked together will not always agree. In such cases a third, unrelated person can be better placed make suggestions that both people can live with – more happily.

Interactivity

The less able a person may be in a particular way, the more they form a focus for another person's livelihood, either as a human resource or in providing a service or product. This applies to every physical or intellectual job, from gardening and building to teaching and accounting. 'Less able' does not have to be due to a recognised disability. It could be that a parent is employed to make parts for cars and does not have time to teach his children, so pays taxes towards someone else being paid to teach his children. Everyone interacts with others.

On a formal level, all skills are traded in the community and the exchange is maintained by some paying others to do a particular job. In turn, these earnings provide taxes as a central source of finance to fund services in the community. Whether disabled or not, individuals recognise that exchanging skills or paying in kind for helping favours allows everyone to retain their dignity, choice and control of what would otherwise be a one-way process. This does not discount those who are generous in their considerations for others and want no return, but it explains that it is often easier to ask for and accept informal help if a gesture of exchange can be arranged and accepted.

S – Society
We all make the rules of our society and we can make it easier for everyone to take part

Rules of society

In a democracy like ours, everybody can have a say in making the rules. Adults select representatives (Members of Parliament) to speak for them in Parliament, where the rules, or laws, are discussed and the representatives decide what is fairest for everyone. Our basic instincts to survive well as animals and as individual people, and our religious beliefs, affect the rules we make. People who do not agree with what is decided can ask their representative to help change the law. In the UK, laws are written down in long documents called Acts of Parliament.

Some laws say how people who hurt others should be punished. Some say what sort of buildings can be built and where. Some allow the government to collect taxes that can be used for schools, hospitals, roads and other services which we all need but which we have to share as they are too difficult to arrange by ourselves.

Laws are a balance of what we think is fair and what we are prepared to pay for in our taxes to provide a way of making them work. They show how we value each other. As our society changes, laws are sometimes altered to reflect the changing needs of all the people in our communities. Although there have been many recent improvements in the ways we help people who are ill or disabled, there are still some groups of people who are not helped as much as they should be in a fair society because their situations are not included in the fine details of the current laws. Disability Rights workers try to improve the laws and how they are used for disabled people.

The most important Acts of Parliament about disability and illness are:

The National Health Service Acts 1946 and 1977. These created and updated a system of free health care, hospitals and low cost medicines for everyone.

The National Assistance Act 1948. This allowed for a basic amount of money to be given to people who are unemployed for any reason.

Mental Health Acts 1959 and 1983. These allowed for most people with mental health disturbances who were in hospital to be helped to live outside hospital and to have more choice in their own treatment and lives.

Abortion Act 1967. This allowed pregnant mothers whose own health would be seriously affected by pregnancy or whose babies would be born with serious physical or mental disabilities, to end the baby's life before it is born naturally.

The Disabled Persons Act 1986. This allowed disabled people to have a say in the design and choice of helping services.

The Children Act 1989. This allowed for children to be considered more carefully as individuals and to have a say in how they are treated in every area of life.

The National Health Service and Community Care Act 1990. This allowed ill or disabled people who did not need to be in hospital to live in their own homes and to be given the help they need at home.

The Disability Discrimination Act 1995. This made it illegal to exclude disabled people from employment, transport, and access to public buildings and services because of their disabilities. Enabling methods such as ramps, alternative formats for written documents, translators and textphones (minicoms) must be made available to those who need them so that they are able to be considered and to perform equally to non-disabled people.

The Carers Act 1995. This allowed help to be given to people who care for severely disabled or ill people at home without pay.

The Education Act 1996. This created a new system of helping children at school who have special educational needs by providing assistants, specialised equipment or teaching to those who find learning difficult or who have physical or sensory impairments, preferably in the school of their family's choice.

The choice of how many and which laws to discuss lies with adults and will depend on many factors, including the maturity of the children in their care. Those who are involved with older children are free to develop these issues within their beliefs or establishment policies as appropriate to their audience.

Laws are about systems, priorities and choices. The underlying principles of mutual fairness, choice, respect and enablement for others can be used to elaborate on all the laws mentioned above but they are particularly challenged in respect to the Abortion Act. This has wider provisions for maternal illness and for babies that are diagnosed as disabled than for other categories. Extensive writings on this may be found elsewhere but adults may wish to call to mind certain factors when discussing this topic, together with euthanasia, eugenics, and genetic manipulations of foetuses.

Even young children can be randomly exposed to these most sensitive and difficult subjects through exposure to inappropriate television and radio programmes. They may start to form their attitudes without the benefit of a balanced adult input.

New scientific techniques are advancing the diagnosis of disabling conditions in-utero and before conception. If current attitudes remain, the future will see many more individual, heart-breaking dilemmas being foisted on potential parents, who will be disadvantaged in making free choices by having unrealistic views of disability and a severe lack of community support.

People born with congenital disabilities before these techniques were available have survived to testify to living full and satisfying lives. Their number, and their influence in reminding society of its real choices, is diminishing with time.

If our community decides to use scientific advances, it must educate children about how to cope with them fairly and in a comprehensively informed manner. If society is to progress and laws are to be respected, support and choice must be delivered in equal measure. Without support there is no choice, only the compulsion of ignorance.

E – Enabled
Disabled people need an environment that lets them do things for themselves.

Enablement

We all use supermarket trolleys to carry shopping. We decide where to take them because we are in charge of them and the floor is level. We don't have to wait to ask an assistant for every item. We see all this as easy and as nothing to do with disability, but the whole system *enables* most people to be independent in choosing what, how and when to buy things for themselves. We forget that someone has arranged for the trolley to be designed, made, placed for our use and collected. We all make use of a wide range of enabling devices without thinking about them as 'different'.

The same applies to other ways which 'enable' people to do things they find difficult, such as a hoist to lift heavy weights at work or in the home, dropped kerbs and tactile pavements to help cross roads, hearing loops, signed video and audiotape notices as well as visible information, all aimed at keeping our environment convenient and stress free for everybody.

Enabling images

Many people think that some enabling strategies are meant only for disabled people. They find them unacceptable because they find disability unacceptable, so they reject the strategy for themselves and others. They themselves use telephones to speak to people they cannot meet, washing machines to save themselves laborious effort and vacuum cleaners to speed up the housework, but because equipment of this kind is so much a part of life it is not regarded as enabling.

Enabling gives freedom

Enabling is a joint enterprise, a team or community activity which puts the disabled person at the centre. In the long term it benefits disabled people and also those who live with them. 'Helping' is more personal, a one-to-one activity with implications of dominance, subjection and exploitation for both helper and helped. Helping is transient and repetitive. It can be quicker and easier to perform a task for someone else than to create a situation in which that person can use their abilities to be independent. Enabling can be more difficult but it has longer term gains. Direct helping will be essential in certain situations, but the possible long term risks should be recognised.

Enabling resources

The variety of enabling resources is restricted only by our limited imaginations. Distinguish between enablement which counteracts disability, and prevention which seeks to stop it being created. When trying to identify possible resources, it can help to consider a range of categories such as the human, mechanical, environmental, attitudinal, animal, technological and medical.

For example, enabling strategies for visual impairment might include :

human	guide, reader, teacher
mechanical	brailled product labels, easy to open containers, white cane
environmental	tactile pavement, bleeping road crossing, tactile indicators on domestic equipment colour contrasts
attitudinal	automatic provision of alternative formats like large print written material
animal	guide dog
technological	speaking battery or electric equipment, voice-activated equipment including computers
medical	removal of cataracts

Prevention might be using goggles, or immunisation against Rubella.

The enabler spectrum

To counteract the damaging notion that some enabling resources are meant only for disabled people, it is useful to devise a spectrum of easily recognised 'enablers' and discuss how various designs avoid total dependence on an individual faculty. Take the example of time: among all the different timepieces you may choose to discuss, include speaking, tactile or vibrating clocks which do not depend only on sight or hearing. Ask what advantages these might have and broaden the discussion beyond their usefulness for visually or hearing impaired people – such as telling the time in the dark, alerting one person among several in a meeting room or when using ear defenders in noisy conditions. Stress the variable degree of our faculties according to different conditions of light or noise. Some people are able to hear or see more than others in a specific circumstance.

Wheelchairs

Although spectacles are probably the most common enabler, wheelchairs are the most easily recognised. They give rise to many unfounded assumptions. Disabled people use wheelchairs and other aids to give themselves the freedom of independent, faster or easier movement. They are not confined to, bound by or in any other way subject to the aid they use.

Some people use wheelchairs whenever they would otherwise stand or walk but more will use them for shopping, sightseeing or sport when the physical effort of walking prevents them from enjoying the event. It is exhilarating to have the freedom to look around instead of having to concentrate on what the feet are doing, or worrying about having enough energy to reach a seat. Many people deny themselves these advantages because they think being seen in a wheelchair will make other people think less of them. This socially bred prejudice has a real impact on their quality of life. Wheelchair users need a relatively flat environment with adequate room. Even those with strong arms and backs will find manoeuvering wheelchairs over long distances very tiring and many prefer powered chairs if they can afford them. This also applies to those who push wheelchairs for other people, particularly if the 'pusher' is also disabled, as may be the case for older couples.

Simulation studies

These rarely reproduce the actual experience of using wheelchairs or any other disability aid, or of everyday experience of the disability itself, but they do give an indication of the energy and skills needed to manoeuvre wheelchairs on uneven or cambered pavements, or paths fouled by animals and litter. Simulation gives a greater understanding of the frustration of being blocked by an avoidable obstruction, such as cars parked on pavements, steps, cramped shops, inaccessible public transport and toilets. People's own homes rarely have enough space to accommodate wheelchairs easily and working surfaces, electrical sockets, window and door catches are commonly situated beyond the easy reach of wheelchair users. Wheelchairs are also subject to punctures and breakdowns and many are unreasonably heavy.

Artificial limbs and calipers

People who have limbs missing through accidents or congenital malformations might use artificial arms or legs to make it easier to walk or handle things, but artificial limbs can be uncomfortable to use. Some people who decide they can manage well enough with alternative methods prefer not to use artificial limbs just to achieve a 'normal' appearance. Calipers are used to support weak legs but they can be too heavy to allow ease of movement. Recent experiments with electronic devices aim to produce systems which will make artificial limbs and calipers move as the wearer wishes, just like ordinary limbs. Advances in lightweight material and textile technology are also helping to create appliances which have vastly improved comfort and appearence.

Y – Young Carers
Everybody cares about their families

When someone close is ill or very disabled, children may be worried or spend more time helping at home and look after themselves more than their school friends do. It may affect their schoolwork and friendships. All children and young people should be encouraged to discuss these types of difficulty with their parents or a teacher.

Young carers are young people under eighteen who are caring for a parent, sibling or other relative who is ill, has a disability, has a mental health disturbance or is affected by HIV/AIDS or substance abuse including alcohol.

Confusingly, 'carer' is also used to mean a person who is employed and paid to assist a disabled or ill person. The following comments refer to unpaid young people who generally live with their disabled or ill parent, sibling or other relative.

Unsupported young carers

Without help, young carers can be affected physically and emotionally. They may risk injuring themselves by trying to lift a heavy person or helping them to move, or become exhausted by disturbed sleep. They may worry about the progress and outcome of a relative's illness and whether it will affect them too. They may have problems at school because of tiredness or absenteeism. They may worry about what situation will meet them when they get home each day, or be unable to study as much as they need to, which can affect their career prospects. They may become socially isolated from their peers for want of free time or the chance to attend social activities, or be embarrassed about bringing friends home, or find that their peers do not understand their situation.

Without appropriate support, young carers may take on nursing duties such as helping their relative to wash and dress, eat and use the toilet. When the relative is an ill or severely disabled parent, the young person might clean, cook or shop for the family and care for other members of the family. They might supervise medicines, manage the family finances and provide emotional support for the relative and the rest of their family. At the same time, they may have to deal with the repercussions and additional stress of difficulties between their parents, possibly even to the breakdown of their relationship. There is often no other adult at home regularly enough to share practical tasks or responsibilities or to support the young person.

Family expectations

Reports suggest that children can become 'socialised' into accepting their caring role at a very early age and this may continue if nobody properly questions how the family as a whole is managing its needs. Each family will have a cultural norm which reflects their expectations of the normal helping activities of interactive family members. Sometimes the need for the child to take on caring duties is rare or intermittent, but some families can gradually slide into dependence, often on one child. The child's comments are typically ignored or disbelieved, and practical help not offered in situations when an adult carer would certainly receive assistance. The child might fear revealing the situation, betraying a parent, or that outsiders will intrude onto the family. Sometimes all the family are afraid that the children or the disabled relative may be removed into care or hospital, which is seen as abandonment.

The possibility that even older infants could be involved in an emotional or physical caring situation should be included among the possibilities considered if children and young people appear to be having difficulties at school. An appropriately sensitive policy for managing such situations should be in place at every school.

Caring is not inevitable

Disability in families does not automatically mean that the household's young people are the practical or emotional carers, or that the quality of family life is poor. Most children who have disabled relatives at home are no different to their peers, all of whom intermittently experience circumstances which can be difficult for a variety of reasons.

Disabled or ill parents often take positive steps to ensure their children are not obliged to be carers. Like all other parents, they find a mixture of success and frustration in their efforts to raise their children, but additional support is sometimes essential to reduce the impact on children if they live with a relative who has a severe long term or progressive condition, a terminal illness or addiction.

Whatever their situation, children may need the opportunity to express their concerns safely and to have their circumstances confidentially acknowledged. They should be made aware of and, if necessary, be supported in getting the physical and emotional help they are entitled to.

PART FOUR
Into action

Guidance for teachers

Disability awareness training is about understanding how much our personal and corporate thoughts are based on assumptions, misunderstandings and cultural pressures, none of which we can easily judge for ourselves. If possible, become more familiar with the basic concepts through an INSET disability awareness course. Courses may also include disability equality training which examines the design and organisation of facilities and services to identify how disabled people can have the same opportunities to participate as their non-disabled peers. Courses should be led by specialised trainers who have personal experience of disability (see resources).

Disability awareness is about recognising negative attitudes in ourselves and promoting positive attitudes in all our pupils. It is relevant to but not primarily concerned with improving pupil's self-esteem, and is not directly about how to teach students with identified special educational needs.

Bringing disability awareness to children aims:

- to help pupils develop a sense of individuality with regard to disability in themselves and others

- to help them understand that a variety of solutions can be applied to any situation

- to help them recognise alternative cultural values more positively

When talking to children about disability:

Try to create a comfortable atmosphere which respects and values all opinions.

Try to promote a Spectrum approach. This emphasises that graduations of ability are part of a natural range of activity, all of which make up a diverse living society.

Try to foster interactive enabling rather than passive 'helping'. Keep in mind the concept of choice for all parties.

Try to develop positive questions and descriptions, for example

'How many different ways can we think of to do X?' and

'Which choices would suit different people best?'

are more positive than

'What would you do if you couldn't do X?' or

'How can you manage if you can't see or hear?'

Use open questions which make demands on children's imaginations and take them beyond the stereotypical level.

Do not try to cover too much disability awareness at once. It is more productive, particularly for younger children, to use the principles described here to inform, explain and expand the normal curriculum subjects than to have 'dedicated' sessions.

Do not expect the burden of explaining to others to be borne by children with personal experience of disability. They may not be able to find words for what is, for them, completely normal. They may be unable to differentiate their experiences from other children's assumptions. Consider talking in advance to any of the children in your class who might be embarrassed by discussing disability. Much will depend on how the session is handled, and the feedback received during the discussion. Raising the topic fairly regularly will make it more familiar and so progressively more manageable for all the children.

Guidance for parents

Discussing disability with your child can feel artificial. If you are disabled yourself, it may raise the profile of something which really isn't that important in your life, or draw attention to differences which you have learnt to ignore.

It's easy to assume your children know about disability or illness, but they won't know all they need to know unless they are told. If someone in the close family is disabled or ill, you will probably be happier if it is first discussed within the family. If you don't give children a chance to approach you, they may imagine it's a taboo subject, one they must cope with alone, no matter how much it may worry them (often without cause). If you take the initiative, you can tell them how it is for you, and give them a base to work from which reflects your family values. You will be confident that the children know they can come back and talk to you again if they are worried in the future.

Using children's books helps to reduce anxiety and embarrassment. You can control the degree to which discussions become personal by returning to the story when you want to, or if the children become bored.

Choose a comfortable, quiet time when you usually read with your child during the day. This allows them to respond quickly with questions which they might dwell on otherwise. Don't make a big issue of the discussion. The best overall approach is to talk about disability as just a part of life, not the be-all-and-end-all.

First read through the book with your child as usual. Help them enjoy the story, ask them what was funny etc, and explain any new words. Ask them some of the questions suggested here, to introduce various topics, but adapt the questions to your own situation. Not everything suggested will be appropriate to your family but a wider knowledge of other disabilities may help your child understand if or how disability affects the way you live compared to other people, what matters and what doesn't.

Keep it simple. Be guided by your child's age and understanding. Explain both the social and medical aspects of disability at a level your child seems happy with, if this is not already obvious to them. Try to illuminate but not to overwhelm. If you refer to parts of the body that cannot be seen, it may help to ask your child's teacher or local librarian to recommend a factual biology book with appropriate illustrations. Another starting point might be the booklets some disability organisations have written specifically for children. Try to use the right word. Children familiar with 'Tyrannosaurus rex' can handle most medical names. Be truthful but most importantly be approachable.

Detailed book reviews

The books here have been selected to show the wide range of texts which can be used to promote discussions about disability. They fall into three main categories:

- those with nothing obviously connecting them with disability but which can be usefully adapted by exploring a different perspective. These are multifunctional and extend the range of class resources.

  e.g. *Winnie the Witch, Elmer on Stilts, Truckers.*

- those which feature a character who is disabled but whose disability has no impact on the story. These are rare.

  e.g. *Seal Surfer, Boots for a Bridesmaid.*

- those which feature major characters whose obvious disability is an important strand of the story.

  e.g. *Stumpy Toe, Precious Potter, The Man, Charlie's Eye.*

Each story is summarised in a way that highlights the disability issues that can be pursued. In the detailed reviews, a range of questions is suggested whose answers can be drawn from the elements of the DICSEY Code as indicated by the preceding initial. Prompts give additional details to help clarify issues which may be found in the story. Connections indicate broader subjects into which the issues covered in the story could be incorporated, mainly for more mature students.

Some questions and prompts may raise issues which are normally considered too subtle or sophisticated for younger children. Suggesting them is a deliberate challenge. It is intended to show that some of the books children read are potent in creating complex attitudes about disability and illness at a very early age. Issues occur at random within the list and can be located by using the summary in the index section. These examples suggest how all sorts of books can be used to raise awareness of disability related issues *with* children. They are *not* necessarily recommended for independent lone readers. Issues of gender, race and age bias will be found in this selection but are not a primary focus here. Advanced readers might be encouraged to consider how the various attitudes expressed in each book interact.

The detailed reviews are followed by a mini-review section which gives brief summaries and comment. In both sections the books are arranged in order of broadly increasing reading age to assist those who are not familiar with the titles. They are classified as

* early reader picture books

* easy reader picture books

* picture books for older readers

* books for fluent readers

* books for fluent mature readers

The first book, *Winnie the Witch*, is presented slightly ahead of its order because at the time of writing, it is the only listed book that is available in Big book format (33cm x 43cm) to facilitate group story sessions, as well as the original 20cm x 28cm size.

Finding the books

Most of these books are available through booksellers or libraries and the most current details are given, but the book market is such that some will soon be dropped from publisher's lists. Some are known to be out of print and available only through libraries. These, and some distributed originally in Australia, New Zealand, Canada and the United States, are included because they exemplify unusual and exceptionally useful story lines, styles or illustrations, and may alert adults to the possibilities in similar stories published in the future. The resource section indicates possible UK suppliers.

Overall method

The detailed reviews show how the DICSEY code can be applied to specific texts. Choose a few books you can easily obtain and examine how each element of the DICSEY code is expressed within the text or illustrations. To avoid some entries becoming unwieldy, not all elements are highlighted in every book.

Consider what each book says about the wider definition of disability, about image, control, society's rules, enablement and young carers. The same process can then be applied to any other story in any format, and to factual texts.

■ *Winnie the Witch* by Valerie Thomas

Illustrated by Korky Paul.
1989 Oxford University Press ISBN 0-19-272197-6
Early reader picture book – *Winnie the Witch* is also available as a Big Book,
on CD Rom and with an activity book.
See also mini-review *Winnie in Winter.*

Winnie and her black cat Wilbur live in a dark ramshackle black house with lots of
stairs. Sometimes Winnie just can't see Wilbur. She falls over him and decides to
use her magic to make his fur green, but then she falls over him in the grass. She
makes him multi-coloured but he is miserable. She thinks again, restores him to
black and makes her house multi-coloured instead.

Questions

D   Why can't Winnie see well enough to spot Wilbur when everything is
the same colour?

E   How can we make things easier to see?

E   Does Winnie use her glasses all the time?

D   Why does it matter if you fall down?

C I Why is Wilbur miserable when he is multi-coloured?

E   How would you change Winnie's house if you lived there?

Prompts

It's better to change the man-made environment than to try to make people
adapt in ways that don't suit them.

People 'see' in different ways: it can help to increase light, improve colour
contrasts, enlarge print sizes and provide tactile information.

Use ramps or lifts instead of stairs, dryers instead of washing lines, and install
bannisters.

Accidents can cause illness or disability which we usually recover from, but
sometimes they damage parts of us that do not mend. They are preventable.

We need to talk to the people we live and work with to take account of
everyone's views.

Connections

Light, visual impairments, structure of the eye.
Care of animals.
Prevention of accidents by design, safe working, education.
Being different, what we are taught to expect as normal, social customs.
Body language, assertiveness, communication skills.

■ Elmer – The Story of a Patchwork Elephant
by David McKee

1990 Red Fox ISBN 0-09-969720-3

Early reader picture book

Elmer the patchwork elephant is different. He is unhappy because he thinks the other elephants are laughing at him. He leaves the herd, disguises himself to look grey like the others and returns to find the herd very solemn, but when he shouts 'Boo', the elephants laugh and say 'That must be Elmer.' When he gets wet, his disguise washes away and he returns to his natural colours.

Questions

D I Why was Elmer different?

D Can it be good to be different?

S Why was Elmer pleased the herd didn't recognise him?

I How did the herd know the new elephant was Elmer?

S Were the elephants laughing at Elmer, or with him?

Also by David McKee:

Elmer on Stilts 1994 Red Fox ISBN 0-09-929671-3

The elephant hunters are close, following the herd by its tracks. Elmer suggests making stilts with backward facing feet to confuse them and the elephants use a ramp to get on the stilts. The plan succeeds and the herd is left in peace... to play with the stilts.

Questions

E How did the stilts help to confuse the hunters?

DE Why did the elephants use a ramp?

I Why didn't the hunters look up to see the herd?

E What can we use ramps for?

Prompts

Aids can be attractive and fun to use but they are tools, not toys, because they are usually essential.

Connections

Physical access.

Tools as enablers.

Design of everyday items for ease of use.

Wildlife and conservation.

■ *Little Blue Car* by Gwen Grant

Illustrated by Susan Hellard
1994 Orchard ISBN 1-85213-640-5
Early reader picture book

The little blue car escapes from the car factory and goes for a day at the seaside. He becomes cold and lonely, wet and frightened, but passing buses, lorries and tractors tell him how to manage so that he gets back safely.

Questions

C Why did the blue car want to leave the others?

D Why didn't the blue car know how to manage on his own?

SE Who could help us learn how to manage?

D Why are different vehicles suited to different jobs?

E What would we need on a day out?

Prompts

People who are suddenly disabled often find they don't know anything about how to cope and need to be given very basic information.

Some disabled people are reluctant to go to new places because they aren't sure if they will manage unexpected obstacles or difficulties. Most trips take a great deal of preparation.

Connections

How cars work, petrol and batteries, and comparisons to healthy eating.
Maps, disability access guides, people who help.
Alternative ways to drive cars or work machines.
Use of computerised or alternative mechanical systems in cars.

■ *Butterfly Kiss* by Vicki Churchill

Illustrated by Charles Fuge
1997 Hodder Children's Books ISBN 0-340-68614-6
Early reader picture book

Ant and Caterpillar eat leaves together until Caterpillar forms a cocoon. When Butterfly emerges, she can't eat leaves and becomes hungry. Various creatures try to help. Worm says she must find the right things for her new mouth to eat and Cat tells her she can fly, but Bumblebee shows her how to drink nectar from the flowers.

Questions

Y Why was Ant worried when Caterpillar didn't eat?

D I How did Ant know Caterpillar and Butterfly were the same friend?

E How did Butterfly find out she could fly?

E What made it easy for Butterfly to drink from the flowers?

C What exchange did Butterfly make with each flower?

E How can we find out what suits us best?

Prompts

Dealing with sudden changes of ability and appearance.

Different creatures try to help by saying what's best for them but Butterfly has to find what suits her own particular needs.

Spectrums, interactivity.

Connections

Life Cycles
Diets
Adaptation.

■ *Something Else* by Kathryn Cave

Illustrated by Chris Riddell
1995 Puffin ISBN 0-14-054907-2
Early reader picture book

Something Else is not like everyone else. He knows this because everyone else tells him and sends him away. When a different something turns up, Something Else is not sure he wants to be friends till he remembers how everyone treated him. Something Else and Something become friends and when a really weird human creature arrives, they make room for him too.

Questions

I Why does Something Else think he is different?

S Why does everyone else send Something Else away?

S Does anyone care about what happens to Something Else?

DIS Why does Something Else decide to like Something?

S Is it all right for Something Else and Something to live apart from everyone else?

Prompts

Everyone else looks clever. What factors affect the visual and audible perception of intellectual or other abilities?

Education is especially important when some opinions are weighted more than others.

Disabled people need to know about disabilities other than their own.

When will Something Else and Something join up with everyone else? Inclusion with other excluded people is not inclusion!

Connections

New political alliances, segregation, ghettoes, inclusion of minorities, cultural variety. Social groupings and strength in numbers.

Emotional need for acceptance and peer pressure.

Creativity versus appreciation in arts and sport.

■ *What Newt Could Do For Turtle* by Jonathan London
Illustrated by Louise Voce
1998 Walker ISBN 0-7445-5493-4
Early reader picture book

Turtle saves Newt from the swamp predators. Newt wants to do something for Turtle but finds it difficult because he is very small. When Turtle is turned on his back by a Bobcat, Newt uses a pole to lever Turtle back onto his feet.

Questions
S   Why were Turtle and Newt such good friends?

C   Why did Newt want to do something for Turtle?

E   How was tiny Newt able to help big Turtle?

D   What can newts do that children can't do?

Prompts
Differential abilities, reciprocating help, tools as enablers.

Connections
Seasons, life cycles, adaptation.
Predators, swamps as a different environment.
Levers.

■ *Helpers* by Shirley Hughes
1992 Red Fox ISBN 0-09-992650-4
Early reader picture book

Children help the male baby-sitter while Mum goes out. Useful for discussing various forms of enablement, and to open conversations about personal helpers in the home or children's concerns about parents going to work or to hospital if appropriate.

Prompts

Domestic scenes.
Keep floors clear, put things where they should be.

Kitchen: audible signals on toaster, clocks and cookers.
Tipping supports for pouring hot liquids and other cooking aids.

Use trolleys to carry crockery etc, washing machine to wash clothes. Large print or tactile message card for milkman. Use reins for baby.

Bedroom: enough room for wheelchairs.
Side-hinging cots for parents who use wheelchairs, intercom to hear crying babies can be linked to vibrating or flashing light alarms.

Bathroom: non-slip surfaces, hoists, thermometers and audible sensors to test water heat.

Television: subtitling, video, Ceefax, cable shopping, education and other services.

Reading: large print, audiotapes, Braille etc

Outside:
Shop: prams/ wheelchair access, moving round inside, finding things.

Park: using alternative senses to 'learn' where everything is.
Safe designs of play equipment and soft surfaces to prevent accidents.
Access to toilets, seats. Sensory gardens.
See also Charlie and the Big Chill *by Lennie Henry.*

■ Charlie and the Big Chill by Lennie Henry

Illustrated by Chris Burke
1995 Victor Gollancz ISBN 0-575-05938-9
Early reader picture book with dramatised audiotape including sound effects and dancing music.

Charlie hates shopping with her mother, but changes her mind after an adventure with the Snow Giant and the ice cream characters. A superbly enjoyable example of the extra dimension of sound effects, but this book and audiotape might be difficult to obtain.

Questions

E How many ways are there of carrying shopping?

E How do we find things we want in big shops?

E How do we know what to buy?

D Does everyone dance as much as Charlie?

I Why does the Snow Giant seem fearsome?

E What sounds help us know what's happening?

Prompts

Use of spectacles on Snow Giant to increase fearsome appearence.

Alternative formats, newspaper tapes, transcription services.

Everyday activities like shopping can present particular challenges for people with disabilities because several abilities are needed at the same time.

Considerations might include the following:

Mobility and dexterity: back-saving high level trolleys (well serviced) adapted for wheelchair-using shoppers and children, wide aisles, reachable shelves, easy open packaging and unit weights. Transport, car parking, driving adapted cars, design of buildings. Shopmobility schemes.

Visual: learning layouts to find things, large print information on signs, price labels, guide dogs.

Hearing and speech: alternatives to information on tannoy systems, interference of background noise and music to hearing-aid users, evacuation alarms, sympathetic hearing scheme, hearing dogs.

Learning: choosing items, reading labels, budgeting, counting money.

Connections

Retail services, home shopping catalogues and IT marketing.
Social infrastructure of transport and distribution.
Packaging design technology. Finance. Commodities.

■ *Cleversticks* by Bernard Ashley

Illustrated by Derek Brazell

1993 Picture Lions ISBN 0-00-663855-4

Easy reader picture book

Ling Sung doesn't want to go to school because everyone else is clever at doing things that he can't, like writing their names and tying laces. One day he uses paintbrushes as chopsticks and finds nobody else can. He shows everyone how to eat with chopsticks and all the children show him how to do what they're best at.

Questions

ISE How did Ling Sung know about chopsticks?

E What other ways are there to eat food?

E How many different ways can the children do up their clothes?

How many different things in the school have wheels on?

How many different ways are there for the children to find out?

How many different ways are there to carry things?

E Who else could use these things easily?

Prompts

Fingers, knives, forks, spoons, straws (space travel and illness), feeding cups, intravenous drip, capsules, tablets.

Laces, buttons, buckles, braces, velcro-tabs, zips.

Scooters, barrow, trikes, railway carriages, computer table, pram.

Books, number notices, computer, tape recorder, coloured labels, camera, weigh-balance, speaking, signs (pointing, gestures), newspapers.

Jars for paintbrushes, barrow, railway carriages for people, trays of paint, clips for paper on easel, backpack, lunchbox, baskets, plant bucket, bath for water, plate, pot for paint, fishtank for water, tray for books, cannister for pencils, chest for books, spade, pan and trough for sand, trough for bricks, pram for baby, gutter for rain.

■ *You and Me, Little Bear* by Martin Waddell

Illustrated by Barbara Firth
1999 Walker ISBN 0-7445-6721-1
Available in Bengali, Chinese, Punjabi, Somali, Urdu, Vietnamese.
Easy reader picture book

Little Bear wants to play but Big Bear has to tidy their cave and get the supplies.
They work together then Little Bear plays on his own till he finds Big Bear asleep.
They play Hide and Seek together and then go home.

Questions

Y What sort of jobs does Little Bear help with?

Y What jobs can he do on his own?

E What other ways could Big Bear find wood and water?

E What makes it easier for us to get water and keep warm?

D Why did Big Bear fall asleep?

Y Who helps to look after us?

Prompts

Discuss how much we all help in the home and what is reasonable and safe for young children to do alone.

Touch and hearing supplement sight to find sticks and water. Understanding the importance of Homecraft is essential in judging how to enable people to live independently at home.

Everyone gets tired after work. Parents and others who have disabilities may get more tired and sometimes they ask other grown ups to help.

Connections

Types of jobs, houses, ways to cook and keep clean with particular emphasis on 'disability' aids to enable domestic chores: vacuum cleaners, washing machines, lightweight easy-grip tools.

Use of sound and light to instruct electrical gadgets to work.

Lone parents.

Gender stereotyping of Young carers.

■ The Man Whose Mother Was A Pirate by Margaret Mahy
Illustrated by Margaret Chamberlain
1996 Puffin ISBN 0-14-055430-0
Easy reader picture book

A respectable little man takes his pirate mother in a wheelbarrow on holiday to the seaside. On the way he meets a stay-put farmer and a miserable philosopher who try to discourage him, but when he gets to the beach he is delighted by what he finds. They are hired by a ship's captain and go off to sea together.

Questions
I   What is respectable?

I   Why didn't Mr Fat ever go to the seaside?

E   Why did the little man make do with the wheelbarrow?

I   What was the song in the back of his mind?

I   Why was the little man surprised about the sea?

Prompts
People adapt to different lifestyles. They are often hampered by fear of the unknown and settle for the 'ordinary'. If they are disabled, it is easy to be discouraged by others who have never tried to break out of their stereotyped role or really aim to achieve their ambition.

Visual stereotypes. Pirates without eyepatches or amputations seem friendlier than those depicted with them.

Connections
Healthy eating.
Ships designed for different uses.
Names as labels.
Hidden disabilities.

■ *Five Minutes Peace* by Jill Murphy

1998 Walker ISBN 0-7445-0918-1
Available in Bengali, Chinese, Punjabi, Somali, Turkish, Urdu and Vietnamese
Easy reader picture book.

Mrs Large the elephant is dismayed at the mess her children make at breakfast. She goes for a bath, telling them play on their own and to look after the baby, but they all sneak into the bathroom. She gets out, and goes back to the kitchen for a few minutes peace before they join her there again.

Questions

D   Why did Mrs. Large want some time to herself?

D   Why is it dangerous to spill food and leave toys on the floor?

E   How did Mrs. Large butter her toast?

E   What can be done using feet and mouths instead of hands?

S   Does Mrs. Large still love her children?

Prompts

Invisible disabilities.

Relaxation and complementary therapies can help energy-sapping conditions.

Alternative methods: wholly hand or foot controlled cars, wheelchairs, writing with feet, mouth operated suck-blow devices.

Use domestic scenes of kitchen, bathroom, stairs and door handles.

Parent-craft, healthy eating.

Connections

Design of home and contents.
Alternative medicines.
Food hygiene and preparation.

■ *Keeping Up with Cheetah* by Lindsay Camp

Illustrated by Jill Newton
1993 All Books for Children ISBN 1-85406-170-4
Available in Arabic, Bengali, Chinese, Vietnamese and Gujarati.
Easy reader picture book

Hippopotamus laughs at his good friend Cheetah's jokes but he can't keep up with him when they run. Cheetah finds other friends to run with but they don't laugh at his jokes. Hippo tries to run faster but he can't – so he goes for a wallow in mud instead. Cheetah says that's dirty, but he misses someone to laugh with him and returns to play with Hippo.

Questions

D Why was Cheetah cross with Hippopotamus?

I Why did Hippo want to cry?

EC Why do Hippo and Cheetah have different ways of keeping cool?

E Are hearing and listening the same?

SE How could Cheetah have told his jokes so that Hippo could hear them?

Prompts

Everyone is good at something but nobody is good at everything. It's good to try hard to do difficult things but trying different tasks might show we have other skills.

Disability can be frustrating if ways are not found to enable everybody to have the same opportunities.

Exploring alternative ways of communicating can be useful if we cannot hear all the sounds that most people can hear, or they cannot hear us.

It is important to have friends we can laugh with, but it's all right to be different too.

Connections

Sign Languages.
Hearing and communication aids, including standard communication devices and their adaptation.
Sound waves and their applications.
Animal communication methods.
Different languages.

■ *John Brown, Rose and the Midnight Cat* by Jenny Wagner

Illustrated by Ron Brooks

1985 Puffin ISBN 0-14-050306-4

Easy reader picture book.

John Brown the dog and widowed Rose live happily together. A black cat comes to the window and Rose wants to let it in, but John Brown resists, foiling Rose's attempts to include the cat. Rose takes to her bed and doesn't get dinner for John Brown, and he worries about her. When he lets the cat in, she recovers.

Questions

Y Was John Brown able to help Rose with everything?

EI Why didn't he want the black cat to come in?

D Why might Rose have become so ill?

D Are disabled people always ill?

I Are old people always ill or disabled?

E What can animals do for people?

Prompts

Rose may have an invisible disability which affects her intermittently or when she is worried or tired. She lives happily most of the time but will sometimes need help from outside the home to prevent crises or to assist if she has a relapse, especially if she lives alone or with young children.

Many people are wary of new, imposed elements in family life. Some children resist help that interferes with their accustomed ways, which reflect on their ability to cope or interferes in the child-parent relationship. Really useful help takes account of this.

Connections

Living alone, bereavement.

Natural body changes and maintaining abilities in old age.

■ *The Three Legged Cat* by Margaret Mahy

Illustrated by Jonathan Allen

1994 Puffin ISBN 0-14-054963-3

Easy reader picture book.

Tom, the three-legged cat, longs to see the world but Mrs. Gimble wants a stay-put cat which doesn't need feeding. She worries what the neighbours will say when they see her being visited by her eccentric travelling brother Cyril, whose hat looks much like curled-up Tom. A fortunate mistake sends Tom around the world perched on Cyril's head.

Questions

D Why was it difficult for Tom to prowl around?

D Why did Mrs Gimble use spectacles?

E How did Tom and Cyril enable each other?

I Why did Tom think the sea was pink?

C Why was Mrs. Gimble pleased Tom couldn't prowl around?

Prompts

Partial disability. Tom could manage to walk short distances at home, but could not walk far outside.

Mrs. Gimble was shortsighted. Discuss its cause and other common forms of visual impairment, and the stereotypical image of spectacles as frumpy.

Enablement is easier if it is a two way process.

Connections

Appropriate clothing and eating.

What we expect to see in other countries and how we find out without going there.

■ *Boots for a Bridesmaid* by Verna Allette Wilkins

Illustrated by Pamela Venus
1995 Tamarind ISBN 1-870516-30-3
Easy reader picture book

Cricket-loving Nicky is to be a bridesmaid but doesn't like frilly dresses or satin shoes, and flowers give her hay-fever. Her Mum makes just the right sort of dress for her and helps her find super red boots to match. The illustrations show that Nicky's Mum uses a wheelchair. Their bungalow home is adapted with ramps, low work surfaces and high-level electric sockets. Mum drives a car with the wheelchair stowed in the back and does everything Mums are expected to do. Disability is not mentioned in the text. It is a superb example of a skillful use of illustration to convey a positive message, as well as en-riching a highly readable story. Nicky's parents are also shown to be of dif-ferent ethnic origins. Published with the Spinal Injuries Association who provide a short appendix on spinal injuries.

Questions

E   Why do people use wheelchairs?

E   What makes Nicky's house easier for her Mum?

E   How can cars be driven without using feet?

■ *Also by* Verna Allette Wilkins: *Are We There Yet?*
Illustrated by George McLeod and Lynne Willey,
1995 Tamarind ISBN 1-870516-29-X
With the Spinal Injuries Association.
Early reader picture book

Max and Amy, aged about six, go for a day at a theme park with Dad. Illustrations show that Dad is a lone parent who uses a wheelchair. He prepares the food, drives, takes the children all round the park, gets his wheelchair onto trains and some fairground rides. Illustrations of a day out complement the simple text, which does not refer directly to disability.

■ *And So They Build* by Bert Kitchen

1995 Walker ISBN 0-7445-3644-8
Easy reader picture book, factual.

Beautiful illustrations show the inventiveness and less familiar abilities of twelve creatures when building their homes. They use whatever is available to create structures that suit their needs.

Questions

E   Do different houses suit different sorts of people?

S   What do we need in our homes?

D   Do people use sticks for different jobs?

Prompts

Physical access inside houses, bungalows, flats, lifts, stairlifts, room to use wheelchairs, ramps.

Support sticks: walking sticks and crutches.

Information sticks: red and white canes used by people who are both deaf and blind, long white canes by visually impaired people.

Tool sticks: with hooks for reaching and grabbing things, brushes, feather dusters etc, shepherd's crooks, truncheons, conductor's batons, marching bandleaders.

Symbol sticks: Black Rod, sceptre.

Connections

Materials technology, design. Biological adaptation.

■ The Legend of the Indian Paintbrush by Tomie De Paola

1990 Hutchinsons ISBN 0-09-176342-8

Easy reader picture book

Native American legend about the origin of colourful wildflowers in Texas. Little Gopher's parents worry that he can't run and wrestle like other boys. When the men go hunting, Little Gopher makes toys and colours them with natural pigments. He paints pictures of the life of the village but dreams of creating the colours of the sunset. One day he finds red and orange plants growing and he uses them for paint. The people celebrate him as 'He That Brings The Sunset to the Earth', and the plants remain to flower every spring.

Questions

Y   Why were Little Gopher's parents worried?

D   Will he live like other children if he is small?

S   Was his art important to the tribe?

E   Would he have discovered his 'gift' if he hunted like the other boys?

E   Why is it important to have pictures?

Prompts

People who are disabled are not necessarily gifted at other activities and should not be expected to excel at something in order to compensate. The potential to develop alternative skills exists in almost everyone, but many of us lack the opportunity to express them.

There are many ways one can make valuable contributions to the community.

Use of oral versus written or drawn material. Alternative formats.

Racial stereotypes.

Connections

Appreciation of art in different cultures.

Technology in making traditional or new colours and fabrics.

Interactive communities.

Environmental issues.

Genetics, inherited disabilities, gene therapy and engineering for new plant and animal characters.

Nutrition, hormones, vitamins.

Mystical visions, spirituality in different cultures.

Creativity – effects and hazards of hallucinogenic drugs.

Life skills and parenting.

■ *Precious Potter, The Heaviest Cat in the World*
by Rose Impey

Illustrated by Shoo Rayner
1994 Orchard Books ISBN 1-85213-678-2
Easy reader, cartoon.

Precious is the smallest kitten in a litter and survives because of his Mother's devoted care. He grows, eats everyone's food, and eventually his father and siblings leave the household. With no income, Precious has to find a job, but he is so heavy that equipment collapses under him. He despairs that nobody will employ him, until Mr. Circus-owner finds him and promptly makes him a circus celebrity, the heaviest cat in the world.

Questions

Y   Why does Mrs. Potter look after Precious so much?

Y   Why do the other kittens and his father feel left out?

Y   Why doesn't Mrs. Potter make Precious share more?

E   Why is it difficult for Precious to keep a job?

I   Why is Precious popular when he is famous?

D   What makes animals heavy?

Prompts

All children in a family have a right to equal treatment. Sometimes in real life, circumstances force attention on a disabled sibling and it can be difficult for tired and worried parents to seem to be equally attentive to their non-disabled children. Help from outside the immediate family may be needed. Young carer issues apply.

Training for employment and independence is essential for everyone. A disabled person might need to find a different way to do a job.

Unusual size can depend on genetics, nutrition, exercise and metabolism, and not necessarily on greed.

It is not helpful to imply that disability is amusing or that fat is freaky.

Connections

Safe exercise, circus skills, disability sports.
Circus history, freak shows, alternative lifestyles.
Parenting and marriage skills, rights to life.
Weight and eating disorders, healthy eating.
Power of advertising and propaganda.
See also Cannonball Simp *by John Burningham*

■ *Cannonball Simp* by John Burningham

1999 Red Fox ISBN 0-09-940077-4

Easy reader picture book

Simp is an ugly abandoned dog that seeks help from the rats, who share their food with him, and the cats who don't. He escapes from the dog warden and finds a circus where he uses his brains, size and shape to help a clown.

Questions

I   Why was Simp dumped as a puppy?

S   How much were the rats able to help Simp?

C   Why was Simp afraid of the dog warden?

E   How was Simp able to repay the clown's kindness?

E   What other ways can dogs help humans?

Prompts

Examine the images of the rats and cats.

Dogs can be trained for specific tasks. In addition to Guide, Hearing, companion and epilepsy warning dogs, there are rescue, sniffer and sleigh dogs.

Connections

Animal welfare, pets and circus

Homelessness, alternative societies, Traveller culture, celebrations.

Uses and dangers of explosives.

■ *Mr. Bear and the Bear* by Frances Thomas

Illustrated by Ruth Brown
1997 Red Fox ISBN 0-09-972611-4
Picture book for older readers

Mr. Bear is a recluse. When he goes into town to repair his spectacles, children ridicule him and he is rude to them. But when he sees a captive dancing bear being abused he is so saddened that he decides to buy the bear and treat it kindly.

Questions

D Why are the children rude to Mr. Bear?

DI Why does Mr. Bear have a reputation as unfriendly?

D Why does Mr. Bear use spectacles?

I Is the bear really dancing?

E What other ways can animals help us?

Prompts

Mr. Bear is partially sighted and may have to concentrate on looking where he is going. He makes less eye contact, which is important to greet people in a friendly way. This is an invisible disability and people often do not understand what they do not see. People laugh at the bear but Mr. Bear notices how it is abused. His judgment is based on past learning and attitude.

There is more than one way to judge any situation.

Reputations restrict the way we react to people. We need to find out for ourselves and make up our own minds.

Adults as well as children ought to have good manners.

Connections

Social communications, body language.
How traditional customs affect our lives now.
Using animals for a livelihood.
Animal vs. human environments, transportation of animals.

■ *All the Magic In the World* by Wendy Hartmann
Illustrated by Niki Daly
1995 Red Fox ISBN 0-09-916021-8
Picture book for older readers

Lena often trips over her own feet and she watches while her siblings climb trees. Joseph, the odd-job man, shows her what he has collected in his special tin: a piece of string to make cats-cradle pictures, a shell hiding the sound of the sea and pull-tops from drink cans making a magic silver chain. When Lena wears this as a necklace she imagines she's a princess, and can actually walk and dance gracefully. Joseph tells the children the magic is found not in tins but in their own imaginations.

Questions
D   Why do the children tease Lena?

D   Why do they think Joseph is silly?

E   How else do the children use their imaginations (pretend)?

E   Would she have found the magic if she'd been climbing trees with the other children?

I   Why do the children seem to be fenced in?

Prompts
Power of confidence.

Appropriate response to strangers, company of other children.

This story is set in Alabama and the illustrations show Lena playing behind flimsy wire fences. This 'fencing in' highlights the use of imagination as a tool in releasing Lena from both disabilist and racial restraints.

Connections
Recycling.

Co-ordination and clumsiness in children, development.

History of the struggle for racial equality.

■ *Stumpy-toe* by Jenny Alexander

Illustrated Caroline Crossland
1995 Hamish Hamilton ISBN 0-241-13517-6
Picture book for older readers

Stumpy-toe is a chicken who has only two toes on one foot. She bangs her head, loses her memory and has to find out about herself when she's taken in by a human family. They bring in more chickens to teach Stumpy-toe how proper chickens behave, but the new chickens peck Stumpy-toe and won't let her sit on their perch. She persuades them of her cleverness and bravery, and teaches them her ways instead.

Questions

D Why does Stumpy-toe loose her memory?

D Does everyone learn how to behave in the same way?

D How can we prevent head injuries?

I Why did the other chickens peck at Stumpy-toe?

C Why did she feel she had to be cleverer and braver?

Prompts

People who have had head injuries or brain damage often need to be taught things in very small steps, that most people take for granted.

It is common for recovery from head injuries to be slow, and incomplete.

Memory and concentration are a function of mental health.

Congenital malformations can be caused by genetics, poor nutrition or various types of pollution

Connections

Self-image and disorientation.

Bullying, con-tricks, safety.

Brain and nerves. Learning patterns.

Foetal development, ante-natal care, birthright, rehabilitation.

Comparative anatomy, food chains, reproductive cycles.

■ Maudie and the Green Children by Adrian Mitchell

Illustrated by Sigune Hamann
1996 Tradewind Books ISBN 1-896580-06-8
Picture book for older readers.

This is a 13th century English folk story. Some people call Maudie simple but she finds and protects Sal and her brother, the two green children from distant Merlin Land. A doctor can't explain why they are green, nor save the boy when he becomes ill, but he wants to parade the girl in a traveling fair. The children are taught English by a priest who denies their origin and bans their language. When Sal marries, she is deserted and chased out of town. Maudie, now a mother, looks after Sal's son Ulf until they find a way back over the green river to Merlin Land.

Questions

D   Why does Maudie think she's 'simple'?

I   Why don't people believe that Maudie found the Green Children?

S   Why was bell language banned?

SC Why does the priest think it's all right to beat the boy?

I   Why do some people think Sal is a witch?

Y   How well does Maudie care for Ulf and her own baby?

E   Why does Maudie want to go to Merlin Land?

Prompts

A mature society will be confident enough in its beliefs and systems to accept differences and enable coexistence.

People in authority must be open to fair judgements of new ideas.

Learning about more than just local cultures.

Language is the most powerful communication tool.

Being at ease with the natural environment.

Connections

Learning disabilities, independence and parenthood.

Religious, state and professional authority.

Child abuse.

Language and dialect, origins, influence of mass media.

Banning or disregarding minority languages or views for political reasons or convenience eg Sign language, Gaelic, Welsh.

■ The Man by Raymond Briggs

1994 Red Fox ISBN 0-09-910881-X
Fluent reader cartoon format.

A naked, miniature man who demands to be clothed, fed and cared for, wakes John one morning. His presence must stay a secret, and the Man's needs and fancies test John's resourcefulness. John tries to identify the Man's species and origins; the Man defends his differences and challenges the parameters of normality. John begins to resent being bossed by the Man and they argue about each other's motives and behaviour. When the Man disappears, John is left in sadness.

Questions

D Why does the Man stay with John?

YS How would things change if John didn't keep the secret?

E What adaptations does John invent?

E What can the Man do on his own?

C Why do the Man and Boy argue?

I Why are John's parents worried about him?

Special note. Young carers may readily identify with John. Ensure discussions include how children can get help if they need it.

Prompts

The sudden imposition of caring thrusts responsibility on the child for which he is unprepared. The tensions of caring, and being cared for, are worsened by secrecy that prevents asking for help and advice.

Caring relationships that work require honest discussions to allow everyone to pursue their own lives independently if they wish.

The balance of power should be negotiable.

Dealing with non-standard needs can be expensive.

Connections

Healthy eating.

Cultural phobias, racial prejudice.

Personal finances, opportunities for education and work.

Community's responsibilities for those who assist others.

■ Charlie's Eye by Dorothy Horgan
1998 Puffin ISBN 0-14-038237-2
Fluent reader

Charlie is football captain until Jason ousts her and calls her handicapped because of her glass eye. Nobody tells her what handicapped means and it doesn't seem good, so she asks Old Meg who is 'just a bit wanting'. Meg was raised in an orphanage where she had to recite a poem to prove she wasn't handicapped, or be taken away and locked up for life. Charlie finds the poem too hard to learn. At football, Jason calls her 'worse than handicapped, useless', but after Charlie runs off she becomes the town heroine when she rescues Meg from a fire. Jason says she's their best footballer and he didn't mean it when he called her handicapped.

Questions
D   How much can Charlie see with one eye?

I   What does handicapped mean?

S   Was it fair that Meg would be locked up if she couldn't recite a poem?

I   Why did Charlie think she had to prove herself?

Prompts
Disabled people often have to prove what they can do in situations where non-disabled people are not tested to discover if they can do the same things. Disabled people sometimes feel they have to do better than non-disabled people so as to avoid criticism.

Meg may have a minor learning disability that was not recognised or given constructive support.

When applied to disability, 'handicapped' usually conveys an 'overwhelming loss of any and all ability'.

Try changing Jason's last sentence to 'I didn't think you would be able to play well, but I know better now'.

Connections
Safety in play, with fireworks, responding to fire.

History of caring for people with mental health disturbances and learning disabilities.

Common visual impairments.

Leaving care or family to become independent.

■ Gwerfyl and the Great Plague by Gwenno Hywyn

Illustrated by Bryan Jones
1993 Pont Books, Gomer Press ISBN 0-86383-930-4
Translated from Welsh by Gwenyth Lilley.
Fluent reader.

It's 1349. Gwerfyl never leaves her village because of her crooked leg. When others go to market she churns butter and baby-sits. As the Plague approaches, the village is closed for protection and the children become sentries. When they sneer at Gwerfyl for not being able to run to raise the alarm, her father gives her a horn to blow. She falls asleep on sentry duty and the baby she is tending wanders off but is found outside the village by Hywel, of whom she's secretly fond. Gwerfyl fears the baby will be infected, but instead it is her own sister who dies of plague in the arms of Mallt, the local recluse. At Harvest time, they need to know if its safe to travel to market again and Gwerfyl risks her life to find out.

Questions

SI Why didn't Gwerfyl leave the village?

I Why did she think Hywel would reject her?

D Why was it hard for Gwerfyl to admit she had fallen asleep?

E How did she raise the alarm?

D Why didn't Mallt catch the plague?

I Why did Gwerfyl volunteer to go out?

Prompts

Differences between infectious illness and disability.

When employers require disabled people to be more skilled than non-disabled employees who do the same job, this is discrimination.

Some people think disabled people do not have partners or children.

Villagers did not understand why Mallt, also disabled, was apparently immune from the plague so they called her a witch.

Fear makes people behave badly and disregard how much each individual can contribute to society. They consider Gwerfyl expendable and don't even ask how she will manage to get back with good news. She has to be a great heroine before she is valued.

Connections

History of infectious diseases and vaccines.
Grief, bereavement and depression.
Spirituality.
Bullying, poverty, child safety and parenting.
Welsh and English political history.

■ The Ghost of Grania O'Malley by Michael Morpurgo

1997 Mammoth ISBN 0-7497-2777-2

Fluent reader

Jessy saves her island from an environmental disaster, helped by the ghost of one of her ancestors. Superbly observed passages describe Jessy's experiences with cerebral palsy, and other people's reactions as she fights for the Big Hill.

Questions

E How could Jessy's teacher have arranged to get her to the top of the Hill?

I Why didn't people believe Jessy got to the top alone?

I Why did she prefer to be helped in private?

CI What was her reaction to TV reports?

I Was Jessy a heroine because she saved the hill or because she was disabled?

Prompts

School as an enabling environment.

Parental and caring relationships.

Other titles by Michael Morpurgo include:

Why the Whales Came

1999 Heinemann ISBN 0-435-13047-1

Environmental, with a pivotal character who has impaired hearing.

Mr. Nobody's Eyes

1990 Mammoth ISBN 0-4797-0104-8

A bullied child has an adventure with a monkey which was trained by a circus clown who is visually impaired.

Waiting for Anya

1991 Mammoth ISBN 0-7497-0634-1

A Second World War refugee story that includes a character with a learning disability.

King of the Cloud Forest

1997 Mammoth ISBN 0-7497-2777-2

An English boy becomes separated from his Tibetan mentor as they escape war. The boy is saved by and lives with Yeti-like animals. Each considers the other's abilities to be extraordinary but they learn from and respect those differences. Later, the boy's relatives assume the reunited mentor is culturally and intellectually inferior as he doesn't seem to speak English, but they too learn better.

■ *In at the Shallow End* by Hannah Cole

1990 Walker ISBN 0-7445-1477-0

Fluent reader

Dawn and her sister are on holiday with their estranged father when they meet Michelle, whose young son Daniel has cerebral palsy. Michelle invites them to help with the boy's intensive therapy programme and he walks on his own for the first time.

Questions

E How did Dawn feel without her glasses?

I Why was Dawn embarrassed when she met Daniel?

DC Why did Michelle make Daniel exercise so much?

E How much would it matter if Daniel did not walk?

I What are we told about Daniel apart from his disability?

Prompts

Intensive therapy programmes are contentious because they involve complex motivations and their outcomes are unpredictable. Both parent and child may experience a lifelong sense of failure if the desired aim is not achieved. Parents have a strong instinct to do everything to help their child become more independent and intensive therapy for young children can be particularly beneficial in realising full physical potential.

This has to be balanced against an acceptance that everyone is more than their physical abilities alone. Normal learning, family and social activities are important in creating expectations of a full life, and finding alternative means to achieve it.

Consider what Daniel might think about it, and how the story could end without Daniel suddenly walking.

Connections

How to find out about managing disabling conditions.

The importance of personal freedom to chose how to manage a disabling condition, and the relative costs to society of supporting more expensive choices.

The use of disability as a literary device which gives a neat but unrealistic view of a situation.

■ *See Ya, Simon* by David Hill
1995 Puffin ISBN O-14-036381-5
Fluent reader

Nathan describes the final two years with his schoolfriend Simon who has Muscular dystrophy. A highly readable story of a group of boys, which unobtrusively and realistically includes more than a score of disability related issues. It could be a useful text for a more extensive disability awareness course, particularly for older boys.

Questions
D   Was Simon ill, disabled or both?

C   What was Simon's attitude to knowing he wouldn't grow old?

E   What aids did Simon use to enable more independence?

Y   How were Simon's parents, sister and friends affected?

I   How did Alex react to temporary disability?

S   Why didn't Simon like Telethon charity?

D   Which character shows he might have a hidden disability? (Dyspraxia)

Prompts
Compare with 'The Haunting of Jessica Raven' or 'No Time at All' for similar disability themes.

Connections
Prejudice – AIDS, Cerebral palsy, Spina bifida

Genetic testing.

Spirituality.

Pressures on marriage and parenting skills.

Sexual relationships and disability.

■ *No Time at All* by Susan Sallis

1994 Corgi ISBN 0-552-52813-7

Fluent reader.

Sam, brother Matt and his family move to a new bungalow where the boys hear the noise of a ghostly steam-train at night. When Sam meets Lisa at his new school for disabled children, he finds out about a train crash where the bungalow was built and they discover why Lisa's Grandad won't talk about the accident. Matt describes how everyone reacts to Sam and Lisa's disabilities, and how the ghost train helps him when Sam dies.

Questions

E   Could Sam and Lisa use their wheelchairs in your school?

I   Why did Sam and Lisa sometimes embarrass people who tried to be nice to them?

C   Was Sam allowed to make up his own mind about what he did?

Y   Why didn't Matt tell his football captain about Sam's illness?

IS   How would Lisa's experience help or hinder her if she succeeds in becoming Prime Minister?

Prompts

Explain the difference between Sam's disability which involves a fatal condition, and Lisa's disability which does not.

Examine the use of dialogue, including casual words denoting mental disturbance.

Connections

How would the story have changed if Sam or Lisa had told it?

How could the story be altered to make an adventure serial involving Sam, Matt and Lisa?

■ *The Time Tree* by Enid Richemont

1990 Walker ISBN 0-7445-1447-9

Fluent reader

Two friends play in their favourite tree and become aware of Anne, a girl from the sixteenth century who seems to be deaf. As they encourage her to write, the girl reveals her frustration about how she is considered to be an unteachable 'idiot' in her own time, and how keen she is to learn. Life changes for her and all her family when she returns to her own time with her new writing skill.

Questions

SD Why did Anne's family think she was an 'idiot'?

DY Why were Anne and her family frustrated?

E Are there other ways to communicate?

EIC How did learning to write change Anne's life?

EC How can we enable people with learning disabilities to have a full life?

Prompts

Ignorance and superstition prevent us from finding ways to communicate with all sorts of people. Many people of Anne's time could not read or write. They would all be effectively disabled in our time because our society constantly uses literacy skills.

Alternatives and aids to speech include British Sign Language, Makaton, body language, lip-reading, hearing aids, writing, and forms of information technology.

The importance of having opportunities to learn.

Friendships and change.

Connections

Causes of hearing impairments – congenital, infections, loud noise.

History of personal and social education.

Time dimensions, conservation and interpretation of artefacts.

■ *Dolphin Luck* by Hilary McKay

1999 Hodder ISBN 0-340-71660-6

Fluent reader.

It's Christmas, Mum's ill and everything's chaotic as the children from two neigh-bouring families get into a fast-moving story of mistaken identities and misplaced best intentions. Features a network of caring relationships which explores the line drawn by society which decrees where eccentricity ends and mental health distur-bances begin. Superb dialogue.

Questions

D How many characters in this story are disabled?

Y How many caring relationships are involved?

Y What is the difference between Perry looking out for his brother Sun Dance, and Tilly's daughter caring for Tilly?

D Why didn't Tilly tell the children that she didn't know them?

I Why did Beany think she'd found the Dolphin sword?

Prompts

Mum is ill temporarily with pneumonia. Sun Dance is unpredictable, remote and distracted at times. Mad Aunt Mabel is eccentric but able, Tilly is eccentric but seems to neglect herself.

Each character creates caring relationships with others, including animals, and is cared for by others. The book offers scope to examine the different levels at which society expects family members to care for each other, be they animals, children, those who are ill or vunerable, and if this vunerability is real or defined only by society's conventions.

Connections

Causes and consequences of disrupting communications.

The duties and rights of society to intervene in the welfare of individuals and the rights of individuals to reject the intervention.

■ *Truckers* by Terry Pratchet
1990 Corgi ISBN 0-552-52595-2
Fluent reader

Masklin is troubled about being left to provide for the elderly nomes (sic) in their rural colony. He searches for somewhere easier to survive and they come to a large department store where each department is home to separate communities of nomes. Everything is Under One Roof and only the rebels dare to suspect there is an Outside. When they discover the store is to be demolished, Masklin has to convince them all to work together and venture into the big unknown.

Questions

Y   Why was Masklin annoyed at being left to provide for the colony?

I   Why was it so hard for the Store nomes to accept the existence of an Outside?

I   How well did 'Our Furry Friends' explain to Gurder about foxes?

E   What was Masklin's way of doing impossible tasks?

E   How did Dorcas adapt the lorry and get it to move?

Prompts

'Outside' symbolises the different world as perceived by some people with disabilities and the denial of the main community (the Store nomes) to recognise that there is another existence.

The skills learnt by different cultures and lifestyles can benefit everyone.

Reading increases vocabulary and knowledge and this gives confidence and power, but books cannot teach everything. Talking to people who have experience of a situation can help in gaining an understanding of it.

Connections

Images of different communities created by word and illustration.

Censorship.

Personal qualities, leaders and population management.

Business management.

MINI-REVIEWS

☐ *Mama Zooms* by Jane Cowen-Fletcher
1993 Scholastic USA ISBN 0-590-45775-6
Early reader picture book

Mama zooms around in a wheelchair with her child on her lap and he pretends to be riding on various different forms of transport. A joyful celebration of one of the positive aspects of being a child of a disabled parent. Useful in highlighting that disabled people have normal family lives and that they often look after other people rather than being looked after themselves.

☐ *Winnie in Winter* by Valerie Thomas, illustrated by Korky Paul
1996 Oxford University Press ISBN 0-19-272316-2
Early reader picture book. Also available as a Big Book and with an activity book.

Winnie and Wilbur are tired of the snowy winter. Winnie's spell turns everything suddenly to summer. She upsets all the plants and is invaded by sunbathers. She casts another spell that restores everything to normal and they snuggle up warm and cosy inside. Useful to explore the shock of sudden disablement by accidents, and some of the causes eg jagged tins, climbing on iron railings. Has a smiley pirate snowman with an eyepatch and skull and crossbones.

☐ *Sophie and Jack Help Out* by Judy Taylor
1983 Bodley Head ISBN 0-370-30561-2
Early reader picture book

Everyone in the Hippo family is worried because Papa is poorly in bed and there's nobody to plant the vegetables. Sophie and Jack sow the seeds on their own. The plants grow all mixed up after a great storm, but nobody minds when Papa gets well again. Very useful for discussing disability, illness, recovery and potential young carer concerns.

☐ *A Pig called Shrimp* by Lisa Taylor, illustrated by Jonathan Langley
1992 Harper-Collins Lions ISBN 0-00-664291-8
Easy reader picture book. Also available on cassette.

Gabriel the Ram tells Shrimp the Pig to swim into a river further than he can comfortably manage. When he finds Shrimp has become ill, Gabriel pulls wool out of his own coat, but the bird onlookers don't understand Gabriel and call him mad. Gabriel uses the wool to keep Shrimp warm until he recovers. Useful for highlighting the difference between misunderstanding and true mental health disturbances, and casual use of terms. Ram has good reason for his behaviour, but a young reader might not understand this without help.

☐ *Lucy's Picture* by Nicola Moon, illustrated by Alex Ayliffe
1995 Orchard Books ISBN 1-85213-955-2
Easy reader picture book.

Lucy makes a tactile picture collage for her Grandad who collects her from nursery with his guide dog. Several useful points for awareness of visual impairments.

'Letang' series by Beverley Naidoo. Longman 1994
☐ *Letang's New Friend*
ISBN 0-582-12154-X
Easy reader picture books

Letang arrives in England from Botswana and makes friends with Julie, who uses sticks and sometimes a wheelchair and is visually impaired. They explore a park in the snow.

☐ *Letang and Julie Save the Day* ISBN 0-582-12155-8

The school outing shows Julie using a computer, deciding when to use her wheelchair, using accessible transport and enjoying the open countryside.

☐ *Trouble for Letang and Julie* ISBN 0-582-12156-6

The class hamster escapes. Features name-calling, use of IT, lifestyles, pets, and ability to travel.

☐ *All the Better to See You With* by Margaret Wild, illustrated by Pat Reynolds 1999 Allen and Unwin ISBN 1-86373-336-1
Easy reader picture book

When Kate gets lost on the beach, her family discover she's short-sighted and needs glasses. Good explanation of partial sight.

☐ *Monty's Ups and Downs* by Colin West
1997 Harper Collins (Jets) ISBN 0-00-675207-1
Easy reader short stories

Monty the dog wears glasses. In *Monty and the Raffle*, Simon and Josie borrow Monty's glasses to embellish their teddy for a competition. Monty is fed up, he misses his glasses and disaster strikes as he tries to reach for a cake. In *Monty's Midnight Snack*, he uses an upturned basket to reach into the fridge. Both stories could prompt a wider discussion on the attitude to and use of various aids.

☐ *Seal Surfer* by Michael Foreman
1998 Red Fox ISBN 0-09-972451-0
Easy reader picture book.

A young boy and his grandfather spy a mother seal and her new-born pup on the beach. As the seasons pass they see the pup growing, facing the hazards of the open sea and returning with its own offspring. Illustrations show the boy surfing and climbing rocks, and also using crutches and a wheelchair. This is a rare example of including disabled characters in a natural way.

☐ *Sachiko Means Happiness* by Kimoko Sakai
1990 Children's Book Press, USA. ISBN 0-89239-122-7
Easy reader picture book

A child's experience of her grandmother who is affected by Alzheimers disease, introducing young carer issues.

☐ *Loosing Uncle Tim* by Mary Kate Jordan
1989 Whitman, USA. ISBN 0-8075-4758-1
Easy reader picture book.

Child's account of the death from AIDS of his favourite uncle.

☐ *Not So Fast, Songololo* by Niki Daly
1997 Puffin ISBN 0-14-056352-0
Easy reader picture book

Songololo's Grandmother asks him to go shopping with her in town. Their conversation reflects how some disabled people are challenged by common environments which non-disabled people do not notice. There are useful insights into getting onto buses, being breathless from exertion, speed of normal walking, shopping finance, road safety, and possibly cultural influences on young carer issues. This is set in South Africa during apartheid and includes significant racial discrimination issues, eg car drivers are white and bus passengers black and dolls in a toy shop are all white. Songololo ascribes his Grandmother's slowness to her age rather than to a disability.

☐ *Dad and Me in the Morning* by Patricia Lakin, illustrated by R.G. Steele
1993 Whitman USA ISBN 0-8075-1419-5
Easy reader picture book

A boy with impaired hearing watches the arrival of a beautiful dawn with his father. They use a torch to lipread and sign, emphasizing the significance of sight and observation.

☐ *Jeremy's Dreidle* by Elle Gellman, illustrated by Judith Friedman
1995 Kar-Ben Copies ISBN 0-929371-34-8
Easy reader picture book

When Jeremy's friends make paper dreidles as Hanukkah gifts for their parents, Jeremy makes one from clay with Braille symbols for his visually impaired father. The presentation ceremony is modified to enable his father to take part. Includes the history of Hanukkah and Hebrew braille.

☐ **My Dad** by Niki Daly
1995 Simon and Shuster USA, ISBN 0-689-506201
Easy reader picture book

A father's addiction to alcohol causes anxiety at home and embarrassment at school until a teacher encourages him to attend Alcoholics
Anonymous meetings. Useful to demonstrate the disabling affects of
substance abuse and possible young carer issues.

☐ **Pest Friends** by Pippa Goodhart, illustrated by Louise Armour-Chelu
1997 Mammoth ISBN 0-7497-2750-0
Picture book for older readers.

Minnie is small and shy. She is friends with Maxine, a colourful lively
girl who just happens to be a wheelchair user. Very slight references in
text, a few adaptive hints, but otherwise just day-to-day stories of
ordinary girls at school.

☐ **Name Games** by Theresa Breslin, illustrated by Kay Widdowson
1997 Mammoth ISBN 0-7497-2886-8
Easy reader

Jane hates her name and decides on something more unusual, but so
does the rest of her class. An amusing introduction to the subliminal
images of name stereotypes and discrimination.

☐ **You Can't Say I'm Crazy** by Robert Swindells
1991 Puffin ISBN 0-14-036506
Easy reader

Two spooky stories of unreality and magic. The author uses 'crazy' as
a wholly acceptable explanation for the logically inexplicable.

☐ **Mad Miss Marney** by Michael Morpurgo. From *The White Horse of
Zennor and other stories* 1991 Mammoth ISBN 0-7497-0620-1
Easy reader

Kate finds an injured bird and the nearest help is the forbidden house
whose owner is a frightening 'mad' woman. Useful to develop an
understanding of a social explanation of 'madness'.

☐ **The Giant's Boot** by Charles Ashton, illustrated by Peter Melnyczuk
1996 Walker ISBN 0-7445-4333-9
Fluent reader

Ritchie finds a giant's huge fossilised boot. When his mother becomes ill and stays in bed, his teacher father takes charge and life becomes a chaotic rush. After a bad row they decide time is not all-important. They stop worrying about trying to get everything done. When they see the giant nearby, Ritchie returns his boot. The giant is blind but he knows the area well and helps Ritchie get back home where his mother has recovered enough to get up and cuddle him. Useful to explore a parent's illness from a child's perspective and to show that time is a factor in taking control and learning to cope.

☐ *Just Like Superman* by Clare Bevan
1991 Puffin ISBN 0-14-036441-2
Fluent reader

After Goggles has the hole in his heart mended he goes to mainstream school. His gang gets caught in a Blitz timewarp which shows their individual strengths and weaknesses. This has contextually relevant references to cardiac surgery and dialogue that reflects the casual use of terms for mental disturbances.

☐ *Cool Simon* by Jean Ure
1992 Corgi ISBN 0-552-52707-6
Fluent reader

Simon Ratnayaka lipreads and uses a hearing aid. He joins a new school and makes friends with Sam, the rebel tomboy who wants to play football although nobody will let her because it's a boys' game. Sam has a cousin with a hearing impairment so she has learnt how to speak directly at Simon and can understand his unclear speech. Their adventures in defeating the Zombie gang and protecting the school's pet raise awareness of both deafness and sex discrimination.

☐ **The Mer-Child** by Robin Morgan, illustrated by J. Spicer Zerner and Amy Zerner 1991 The Feminist Press, USA ISBN 1-55861-054-5
Fluent reader

The Mer-Child has a human father and a mer-maid mother. He is fascinated by a girl whose father carries her onto a beach and he encourages her to swim. A relationship forms between them, her legs strengthen and she grows up to be an oceanographer. A short story which touches on differences, belonging, rejection and love, healthy environments and learning from one another. It is powerfully written, with an unmistakable message.

☐ **Sticky Beak** by Morris Gleitzman
1995 Piper ISBN 0-330-33681-9
Fluent reader

Rowena adopts a bad-tempered cockatoo whose escapades are a backdrop to her own life. She worries that her parents will love their new baby more than her because, unlike her, the baby will be able to speak. Her responses to several disability themes are realistically described within an entertaining and thought-provoking story about the uncertainties of growing up with a disability.

Also by Morris Gleitzman **Two Weeks with the Queen**
1999 Puffin ISBN 0-14-130300-X
Fluent mature reader

An Australian boy asks the Queen to send her best doctor to help his brother who has leukaemia. His parents send him to English relatives to avoid the trauma of his brother's death. He befriends a man whose male partner dies of cancer and AIDS, and who helps him return to his family before his brother dies. Pun on 'Queen' could devalue the story for less mature readers.

☐ *Krindlekrax* by Phillip Ridley, illustrated by Mark Robertson
1991 Jonathan Cape ISBN 0-224-03149-X
Fluent reader

'Thin, bespeckled' Ruskin wants to be a hero but he is hampered by ineffective parents who are depressed and alcoholic, and he has also to placate the local bully. He seizes an opportunity to save the street from the Krindlecrax monster. Useful treatment of the caretaker's death, stereotyped images and young carer issues.

☐ *Waterbound* by Jane Stemp
1995 Hodder ISBN 0-340-63477-4
Fluent mature reader

A futuristic story set in a super-regulated society from which all trace of disability has been removed. Gem finds disabled children living in the secret rivers below the City. She learns to question moral issues of foetal screening, rights to life and to knowledge, the power of health professionals and comparative poverty.

☐ *Hero of Lesser Causes* by Julie Johnston
1994 Orchard ISBN 1-85213-678-2
Fluent mature reader

Keely is a lively teenage campaigner for assorted causes. When her brother becomes severely paralyzed from polio in the 1947 epidemic, her energies are challenged. A realistic and readable account of family change. Useful for carer issues, including the feminisation of care for men, and parental response to children being ill. Patrick's journey through anger, loosing the will to live and ultimately regaining normal male adolescent desires offers awareness of the significance of modern immunisation, notifiable diseases which may lead to death or disability and the outcome for survivors.

☐ *Izzy Willy-nilly* by Cynthia Voigt
1987 Collins ISBN 0-00-184423-7
Fluent mature reader

Izzy's story is about her response to becoming a 'cripple' following leg amputation after a road accident. Like her friends and family, she is conditioned to regard disability as an unredeemable disaster, and this is worsened by her school's failure to accommodate her needs properly. A good account of the difficulties which occur when people do not know how to manage disability, but does not reach as far as showing possible solutions.

☐ *The Haunting of Jessica Raven* by Ann Halam
1995 Dolphin Orion ISBN 1-85881-069-8
Fluent reader

Jessica's older brother has a progressive paralyzing condition from which he may die within months. On holiday, Jessica gets involved in a time warp adventure which leads her to a scientist and a cure which might save her brother. This highly readable story describes the practicalities of venturing into unaccustomed places with a wheelchair, and Adam's rather virtuous response to his situation. The literary use of 'cures' that produce unrealistically happy endings is not generally encouraged, but the circumstances of this story indicate that it would be abnormal not to pursue all reasonable possibilities because Adam has a terminal illness, not just a disability.

☐ *Nightwatch* by Errol Broome
1995 * Freemantle Arts Press *PO Box 320, 193 South Terrace, South Freemantle, Western Australia ISBN 1-863681-10-8
Fluent reader

Chippy knows the scenes in her father's paintings not by sight but from the sounds of rain and wind on different building materials, music, scents and the characters who live there. A good example of an action plot combined with descriptions based on sounds, smells and an awareness of space which are stimulating and challenging to sighted readers.

☐ *The Blue Horse* by Norman Silver, illustrated by Jilly Wilkinson
1997 Faber and Faber ISBN 0-571-19055-3
Fluent reader.

Alex is facially scarred in a car accident which also injures his mother, and his parents separate when his father cannot cope with the consequences of the accident. With his grandfather, Alex creates a fantasy story which mirrors his personal journey of learning, how to stick up for himself and about his parent's frailty as individuals. Published in association with Changing Faces, which offers support to people with facial disfigurements.

☐ *The Wormholers* by Jamila Gavin
1996 Mammoth ISBN 0-7497-2583-4
Fluent reader

Three children become engulfed in parallel universes. Sophie finds she is no longer affected by cerebral palsy but is subject to manipulation by a being who wants to use her brilliant intellect. Sophie has to chose between power over other people and control of her own life.

☐ *Tinker's Career* by Alison Leonard
1989 Walker ISBN 0-7445-0844-4
Fluent mature reader

Tina rebels against the secrecy surrounding her mother's disappearance from her life when she was a toddler. Her search takes her to her mother's sister who reveals a family history of Huntington's Chorea, a severe hereditary condition of the nervous system that becomes apparent in early adulthood. This could affect Tina and her Aunt too, but it was not the entire cause of her mother's early death. The book explores Tina's shock, anger and bewilderment, often in strong language. It offers an explanation and a realistic view of the emotions aroused by the uncertainty of this difficult condition.

☐ *The Other Side of Silence* by Margaret Mahy
1997 Puffin 0-14-037803-0
Fluent mature reader

Nobody really knows why Hero chose to stop talking when she was nine. When Hero starts to help the eccentric Miss Credence, she finds Miss Credence's daughter, brain-damaged and chained to her bed, and becomes trapped with her. From an unusual perspective, the book explores the pressures generated by the ability to communicate complex ideas through speech, and the power of deciding not to speak: 'The name was a leash that could be used to twitch me into place'.

RESOURCES

BRITISH COUNCIL OF DISABLED PEOPLE have a national mailing list of Disability Equality Trainers and are working on the development of standards in Disability Equality Training.
Groups Development Manager, BCODP,
Litchurch Plazza, Litchurch Lane, Derby, DE24 8AA
Tel 01332-295551 Fax 01332-295580 Textphone 01332-295581

BRITISH DEAF ASSOCIATION provides signed videos of children's stories, beginner's guide to Sign, posters and books. By mail order from
Forest Book Shop, 8 St. John's Street, Coleford, Glos. GL16 8AR.
Tel 01594-833858 voice and text Fax 01594-833446

CARERS NATIONAL ASSOCIATION includes Young Carer support.
20 / 25 Glasshouse Yard London EC1A 4JT
Tel 020-7490-8818 Fax 020-7490-8824

DEAFBLIND UK
100 Bridge Street, Peterborough PE1 1DY
Tel 0800-132320 Fax 01733-358356 Textphone 01733-358100

DISABLED PARENTS NETWORK supports people who have disabilities in pregnancy and parenting. Contact through DISABILITY, PREGNANCY AND PARENTHOOD INTERNATIONAL. (DPPI),
45 Beech Street, London, EC2P 2LX.
Tel 020-7628-2811 Fax 020-7628-2833 Textphone 020-7256-8899
Freephone Information Service 0800-018-4730

HEARING CONCERN organises the Sympathetic Hearing Scheme and supports people with hearing impairments.
7-11 Armstrong Road, London, W3 7JL
Tel 020-8740-4447 Fax 020-8742-9043 Textphone 020-8742-9151

HEARING DOGS for DEAF PEOPLE Training Centre.
London Road A40, Lewknor, Oxon. OX9 5RY.
Tel 01844-353-898 voice and text Fax 01844-353-099

LETTERBOX Library. Mail order bookclub specialising in non-sexist and multicultural books for children, many imported. Theme lists including disability available.
Unit 2D, Leroy House, 436 Essex Road, London N1 3QP
Tel 020-7226-1633 Fax 020-7226-1768

MENCAP Royal Society for Mentally Handicapped Children and Adults.
National Centre 123, Golden Lane, London EC1Y ORT
Tel 020-7454-0454

MIND National Association for Mental Health.
Granta House, 15-19 The Broadway, Stratford London E15 4BQ
Tel 020-8519-2122 Fax 020-8522-1725

NORFOLK CHILDRENS BOOK CENTRE hold extensive stock and can often obtain books in print from overseas publishers.
Church Lane, Alby Norwich Norfolk. NR11 7HB
Tel 01263-761402 Fax 01263-768167

RADAR the Royal Association for Disability and Rehabilitation works to improve the environment for disabled people, campaigns for rights and needs, challenges negative attitudes and stereotypes, particularly in social services, social security, employment, education, housing and mobility. May be able to suggest suitable disability awareness resources. 12 City Forum, 250 City Road, London EC1V 8AF, Tel 020-7250-3222 Fax 020-7250-0212 Textphone 020-7250-4119

REACH National Advice Centre for Children with Reading Difficulties. The Centre provides advice and assistance relating to reading disability in children and offers a comprehensive resource collection of books and materials. Publications include a Newsletter, Starting Points, Next Steps, and Handbooks.
REACH, California Country Park, Nine Mile Ride, Finchampstead, Berks RG40 4HT
Tel 01189-737575 (voice and text) Fax 01189-737105

RNIB Royal National Institute for the Blind. Works for the welfare of people who are visually impaired. Publishes 'Finding out about blindness' teacher's pack and children's board-game packs, and a video with teacher's notes.
224 Great Portland Street, London W1N 6AA
Tel 020-7388-1266 Fax 020-7388-2034

SANE offers support and information on mental health.
199-205, Old Marylebone Road, London NW1 5QP
Tel 0345-678000

SAVE THE CHILDREN Centre for Young Children's Rights promotes the rights of children up to 11 with particular focus on younger children. Reference library, children's books, toys, educational packs and leaflets.
356 Holloway Road, London N7 6PA.
Tel 020-7700-8127 Fax 020-7697-0982

SENSE, the National Deafblind and Rubella Association.
11-13 Clifton Terrace, Finsbury Park London N4 3SR.
Tel 020-7272-7774 Fax 020-7272-6012 Textphone 020-7272-9648

'UNDERSTANDING DISABILITY' (1995) Video pack and notes produced by disabled people and teachers to help children understand about disability. A copy was sent to all schools for 8-18 year olds in England by the Disability Educational Trust. New copies are not available.

Further reading

The books listed below will be of interest to those wanting to know more about what children learn from their books. In particular, Babette Brown's and Pat Pinset's books provide extensive references to the most recent work for detailed study.

Baddeley, P and Eddershaw, C. (1994) *Not So Simple Picture Books: developing responses to literature with 4-12 year olds.* Stoke on Trent: Trentham Books, ISBN 0-948080-79-5

Brown, B. (1998) *Unlearning Discrimination in the Early Years.* Stoke on Trent: Trentham Books, ISBN 1-85856-122-1

Graham, J. (1990) *Pictures on the Page.* Sheffield: National Association for the Teaching of English (NATE) ISBN 0-901291-20X

Moorcroft, C. (1998) *Responding to Stories – Learning Activities for the Early Years.* London: A&C Black ISBN 0-7136- 48554

Pinset, P. (1997) *Children's Literature and the Politics of Equality.* London: David Fulton in association with Roehampton Institute. ISBN 1-85346-425-2

For updates and information, see website
http/web.ukonline.co.uk/happyeverafters

Index of authors and illustrators

Index of book titles and DICSEY directory

Title	Category	D	I	C	S	E	Y	Physical	Sensory	Mental Health	General	Page
A Pig Called Shrimp	Easy PB	•	•			•	•	•		•		22, 91
All The Better To See You With	Easy PB	•				•			•			92
All the Magic in the World	Older PB	•	•			•				•		77
And So They Build	Easy PB	•			•	•					•	72
Are We There Yet?	Early PB	•				•		•				71
Beauty and the Beast	text reference											9
Boots For A Bridesmaid	Easy PB	•				•		•			•	12, 13, 54, 71
Bubblegum Guy	text reference											6
Butterfly Kiss	Easy PB	•	•	•		•	•	•		•	•	59
Cannonball Simp	Easy PB	•	•	•	•	•		•				15, 75
Charlie and the Big Chill	Early PB	•	•			•		•	•	•	•	63
Charlie's Eye	Fluent	•	•		•				•	•		54, 81
Cleversticks	Easy PB	•				•	•			•	•	13, 64
Cool Simon	Fluent	•				•	•		•		•	95
Dad and Me in the Morning	Easy PB	•			•	•			•	•		93
Dolphin Luck	Fluent	•			•		•		•			29, 88
Elmer	Early PB	•	•	•	•	•		•			•	57
Elmer on Stilts	Early PB	•	•		•	•		•				54, 57
Five Minutes Peace	Easy PB	•			•	•				•	•	14, 67
Gwerfyl and the Great Plague	Fluent	•			•	•		•		•	•	82

Index of book titles and DICSEY directory continued

Title	Category	D	I	C	S	E	Y	Physical	Sensory	Mental Health	General	Page
Heidi	text reference											20, 21
Helpers	Early PB	•				•					•	13, 62
Hero of Lesser Causes	Fluent mature	•				•	•	•		•		97
In At The Shallow End	Fluent	•	•			•	•	•				23, 84
Izzy Willy-Nilly	Fluent mature	•	•			•		•		•	•	98
Jeremy's Dreidle	Easy PB	•			•	•	•				•	93
John Brown, Rose And The Midnight Cat	Easy PB	•	•			•	•	•	•			69
Just Like Superman	Fluent	•	•					•				95
Keeping Up With Cheetah	Easy PB	•	•	•	•	•						68
King Of The Cloud Forest	Fluent	•	•	•	•	•		•	•			83
Krindlekrax	Fluent	•	•	•			•	•	•	•	•	97
Letang And Julie Save The Day	Easy PB	•				•	•	•	•			91
Letang's New Friend	Easy PB	•				•		•	•			91
Little Blue Car	Early PB	•		•	•	•		•				58
Loosing Uncle Tim	Easy PB	•					•	•				93
Lucy's Picture	Easy PB	•				•	•		•			91
Mad Miss Marney	Easy	•	•		•					•		29, 94
Mama Zooms	Early PB	•	•			•		•				90
Maudie And The Green Children	Older PB	•	•	•		•	•	•	•	•		79
Monty's Ups and Downs	Easy	•				•		•	•			92

Index of book titles and DICSEY directory continued

Title	Category	D	I	C	S	E	Y	Physical	Sensory	Mental Health	General	Page
Mr. Bear And The Bear	Older PB	●	●			●			●		●	76
Mr. Nobody's Eyes	Fluent	●				●			●		●	83
My Dad	Easy PB	●	●				●	●			●	94
Name Games	Easy	●	●		●							94
Nightwatch	Fluent	●	●	●		●			●			98
No Time At All	Fluent	●	●	●		●	●	●			●	86
Not So Fast, Songololo	Easy PB	●	●	●	●	●	●	●			●	93
One Eyed Jake	text reference											11
Pest Friends	Older PB	●				●		●				6, 94
Peter Pan	text reference											11, 12, 37
Precious Potter The Heaviest Cat in the World	Easy cartoon	●	●			●	●	●				14, 15, 54, 74
Sachiko Means Happiness	Easy PB	●	●				●			●		92
Seal Surfer	Easy PB	●	●			●		●			●	6, 12, 54, 92
See Ya, Simon	Fluent	●	●	●		●	●	●			●	85
Something Else	Early PB	●	●	●	●					●	●	60
Sophie And Jack Help Out	Early PB	●					●					90
Sticky Beak	Fluent	●	●						●			96
Stumpy-toe	Older PB	●	●	●				●		●		54, 78
The Blue Horse	Fluent	●	●	●			●	●				99
The Famous Five	text reference											7

Index of book titles and DICSEY directory continued

Title	Category	D	I	C	S	E	Y	Physical	Sensory	Mental Health	General	Page
The Bus People	text reference											6, 7
The Ghost Of Grania O'Malley	Fluent	•	•	•		•	•	•			•	8, 83
The Giant's Boot	Fluent	•	•	•		•	•	•				95
The Haunting of Jessica Raven	Fluent	•				•	•	•			•	98
The Hunchback of Notre Dame	text reference						•					7, 9
The Legend of the Indian Paintbrush	Easy PB	•			•		•	•				73
The Little Mermaid	text reference											8, 37
The Lord of the Rings	text reference											37
The Man	Fluent cartoon	•	•	•	•	•	•	•				54, 80
The Man Whose Mother Was A Pirate	Easy PB	•	•			•	•	•			•	11, 66
The Mer-Child	Fluent	•			•	•	•	•			•	96
The Strange Case of Dr Jekyll and Mr Hyde	text reference											20
The Other Side of Silence	Fluent mature	•	•	•	•	•	•	•	•		•	100
The Three Legged Cat	Easy PB	•	•	•				•				70
The Tin Soldier	text reference	•			•	•	•		•			9
The Time Tree	Fluent	•	•	•	•	•	•				•	87
The White Horse of Zennor	text reference											29, 94
The Wormholers	Fluent	•		•		•	•	•			•	23, 99
Tinker's Career	Fluent mature	•		•		•	•	•		•		99
Treasure Island	text reference											11, 12, 17, 19

Index of book titles and DICSEY directory continued

Title	Category	D	I	C	S	E	Y	Physical	Sensory	Mental Health	General	Page
Trouble For Letang And Julie	Easy PB	•				•		•	•			91
Truckers	Fluent	•	•		•	•	•	•			•	54, 89
Two Weeks with the Queen	Fluent mature	•	•	•	•	•	•	•			•	96
Waiting For Anya	Fluent	•				•	•			•	•	83
Waterbound	Fluent mature	•	•	•	•	•	•	•	•	•	•	97
What Newt Could Do For Turtle	Easy PB	•	•	•		•	•	•				61
Why The Whales Came	Fluent	•				•		•	•		•	83
Winnie in Winter	Early PB	•	•									90
Winnie The Witch	Early PB	•	•	•		•		•	•			13, 54, 55, 56
You And Me, Little Bear	Easy PB	•				•	•	•				14, 65
You Can't Say I'm Crazy	Easy	•								•		29, 94